The
Reference
Shelf

Chemical and Biological Warfare

Edited by Brian Solomon

The Reference Shelf
Volume 71 • Number 3

The H.W. Wilson Company
New York • Dublin
1999

The Reference Shelf

The books in this series contain reprints of articles, excerpts from books, addresses on current issues, and studies of social trends in the United States and other countries. There are six separately bound numbers in each volume, all of which are usually published in the same calendar year. Numbers one through five are each devoted to a single subject, providing background information and discussion from various points of view and concluding with a subject index and comprehensive bibliography that lists books, pamphlets, and abstracts of additional articles on the subject. The final number of each volume is a collection of recent speeches, and it contains a cumulative speaker index. Books in the series may be purchased individually or on subscription.

Visit H.W. Wilson's Web site: www.hwwilson.com

Library of Congress Cataloging-in-Publication data
Chemical and biological warfare / edited by Brian Solomon.
               p. cm. — (Reference Shelf: v. 71, no. 3)
      Includes bibliographical references and index.
      ISBN 0-8242-0964-8 (pbk.: alk. paper)
1. Chemical warfare.   2. Biological warfare. I. Solomon, Brian
II. Series
UG447.C515   1999
356'.34—dc21   99-33264
CIP

Printed in the United States of America

Contents

Preface

Throughout the course of the 20th century, the threats of chemical and biological methods of warfare have loomed large. These threats have waxed and waned according to the political climate, and now, as the century draws to a close, they are more of a danger than ever before. Numerous incidents, such as the terrorist nerve gas attack in the Japanese subway system in 1995 and the apprehension of two men in Las Vegas suspected of possessing lethal anthrax bacteria, have demonstrated the very real danger such "alternative" means of warfare now pose. Many of the world's nations are suspected of having significant chemical/biological weapons programs. In recent years, Iraq has become most notable among these for its continued resistance to United Nations inspections.

There are many observers who feel that it is only a matter of time before we begin to see these warfare tactics employed on a large scale. It would not be the first time; Japan used large quantities of germ agents in China in the years leading up to World War II, and in the past two decades, Iraq has made use of both chemical and biological weapons against Iran as well as to quell rebel uprisings among its own citizenry. Those who remain skeptical about the threat of large-scale chemical/ biological attack point out that such materials are difficult to deliver in weapon form, often depending on such tenuous variables as weather conditions. They also stress the dangers such weapons would pose to those who would seek to use them; such dangers would, according to their argument, render these forms of warfare highly impractical.

Often referred to as "the poor man's nuclear weapons," chemical and biological weapons are relatively cheap and easy to manufacture in comparison to atomic devices. Many are capable of causing widespread death without the destruction of property caused by nuclear devices. For these reasons, it is believed that many third world nations as well as terrorist groups in search of weapons of mass destruction within their financial means may turn to biological and chemical weaponry. The products of a growing branch of applied science known as "biotechnology," many types of chemicals and bacterial/viral agents originally designed with positive scientific benefits in mind can be twisted toward destructive purposes with relative ease.

The distinction between chemical and biological weapons is that chemical weapons consist of artificially engineered compounds, while biological weapons consist of living microscopic organisms. Biological warfare, of which germ warfare is a specific type, is the older of the two: instances of its usage can be found in ancient history, such as the Assyrians' poisoning of wells with the fungus disease rye ergot in the sixth century B.C. Living agents of disease add another deadly variable to the equation, in that they are usually communicable, and can spread beyond the target area for an indefinite period of time. Furthermore, biological agents are widely available for legal purposes such as medical research, and can thus be obtained through such commonplace means as mail-order catalogs (it is believed that this is how Saddam Hussein's alleged stockpile was initiated). Chemical weapons such as mustard gas first became a major issue during World War I. Although they must usually be engineered and are non-communicable, chemical agents are typically even more accessible in that anyone with a reasonable knowledge of chemistry can design them, often with no more than everyday household compounds. Despite their more recent emergence, historically speaking, chemical weapons now represent a danger just as real as that of their biological counterparts. Together, they make up perhaps the greatest military threat to the human race as we begin the new millennium.

The purpose of this book is to give the reader a general overview of the state of chemical and biological warfare in the world today, in both potential and actual forms, by presenting recent articles dealing with the subject. The articles are divided into five separate categories, each representing a major aspect or issue connected to the topic. In order to present a wide array of opinions and balance opposing viewpoints, I have attempted to select articles expressing attitudes of both a positive and negative nature, as well as those which simply report current situations as they stand. These views should not be taken by the reader as the last words on these often controversial issues, and I suggest that this volume be used as a starting point for further research.

The first chapter of this book is entitled "History and Background," and offers the reader a look back on the development of chemical and biological warfare over the centuries, as well as in the earlier decades of the 20th century. Among the items included is an important historical document, the protocol established at the Geneva Convention of 1925. In addition to history, the selections in this chapter provide a general summary of recent events involving chemical and biological weapons. In the second chapter, "The Persian Gulf and Iraq," the ongoing problem of Iraq's suspected chemical and biological arsenal is discussed. This chapter also includes two pieces specifically dealing with the so-called Gulf War syndrome reported by many American veterans of the Gulf Conflict. The articles assembled for the third chapter, "The Chemical Weapons Convention" focus on the convention and its proposed ban on the stockpiling of said agents. In this chapter in particular, I have endeavored to present an equal assessment of both sides of this crucial issue. "Terrorism at Home and Abroad" is the fourth chapter, containing articles that explore the ever-growing problem of independent "non-states" (i.e. civilians) gaining the ability to literally wage war with nations such as the U.S. through biological and chemical means. Our final chapter asks the important question "Is the United States Prepared?" Here you will find a number of articles assessing America's capability of dealing with potential chemical or biological attack. As with "The Chemical Weapons Convention," I have tried as much as possible to give both positive and negative assessments.

I would like to thank the following members of the H.W. Wilson General Reference Department: Michael Schulze, vice president of General Reference; Hilary Claggett, senior editor; Gray Young, managing editor; and Beth Levy, associate editor. I am also grateful to the authors and publishers who granted permission to reprint their material in this collection. I additionally wish to thank Christopher Mari, whose helpful suggestions and encouragement were tremendous aids in putting this volume together.

Brian Solomon
June 1999

I. History and Background

Editor's Introduction

Chemical and biological warfare has been with us in one form or another since the earliest days of human civilization. From plague-ridden corpses catapulted over castle walls to mustard gas sprayed over World War I battlefields to anthrax spores cultivated in present-day laboratories, they have taken many shapes over the years. Regardless of the form, these types of weapons have played a major role in military history. The 20th century has seen their development and use escalate higher than ever before, despite ongoing attempts to regulate or ban them. The current world situation with regard to chemical and biological weapons is not unlike the nuclear arms standoff that existed during the cold war.

In order to understand the problem, an overview of its history and background is necessary, and that is what this chapter is designed to provide. The first item included is the Geneva Protocol of 1925. This document was the product of a convention of nations that had met for the sole purpose of dealing with the growing menace of chemical warfare. Such warfare tactics had been a key factor in the World War of the previous decade, accounting for roughly 8 percent of all deaths, and there was a general consensus at the time that something had to be done to prevent such war atrocities from happening again. Note, however, that the protocol's conditions prohibit only the *use* of chemical weapons, not their development or stockpiling. This provided most nations the loophole they needed to keep their arsenals intact, with the unspoken understanding that they could be employed for retaliation.

This section's second article, "Biological Weapons, Literally Older than Methuselah," which originally appeared in the *New York Times*, takes a look at chemical and biological warfare over the centuries, including the century now concluding. Author Judith Miller lists many historical instances of such warfare, such as the 14th-century siege of Kaffa and the spread of smallpox among Native Americans during the French and Indian War. The author analyzes the significance of these historical examples in light of modern-day circumstances. Also included are discussions of attempts to control the use of chemical and biological weapons, such as the aforementioned Geneva Convention.

The section's third article, "The Weapon Too Terrible for the Parade of Horribles," is more concerned with providing background on the present threat of chemical and biological warfare than with discussing the early history of such warfare. Although certain historical anecdotes are presented, Roger Cohen (writing for the *New York Times*) focuses on how these incidents relate to America's more recent problems with chemical and biological weapons. Cohen is mostly interested in the possible danger posed by Iraq's Saddam Hussein. The author attempts to ascertain exactly how real a danger

Hussein represents, and discusses the effectiveness of American measures taken to counteract whatever danger may exist. This article is included primarily for its concise summary of recent issues regarding chemical and biological warfare.

Protocol for the Prohibition of the Use in War of Asphyxiating, Poisonous or Other Gases, and of Bacteriological Methods of Warfare[1]

The undersigned Plenipotentiaries, in the name of their respective governments:

Whereas the use in war of asphyxiating, poisonous or other gases, and of all analogous liquids, materials or devices, has been justly condemned by the general opinion of the civilised world; and

Whereas the prohibition of such use has been declared in Treaties to which the majority of Powers of the world are Parties; and

To the end that this prohibition shall be universally accepted as a part of International Law, binding alike the conscience and the practice of nations;

Declare:

That the High Contracting Parties, so far as they are not already Parties to Treaties prohibiting such use, accept this prohibition, agree to extend this prohibition to the use of bacteriological methods of warfare and agree to be bound as between themselves according to the terms of this declaration.

The High Contracting Parties will exert every effort to induce other States to accede to the present Protocol. Such accession will be notified to the Government of the French Republic, and by the latter to all signatories and acceding Powers, and will take effect on the date of the notification by the Government of the French Republic.

The present Protocol, of which the English and French texts are both authentic, shall be ratified as soon as possible. It shall bear today's date.

The ratifications of the present Protocol shall be addressed to the Government of the French Republic, which will at once notify the deposit of such ratification to each of the signatory and acceding Powers.

---

1. From the Geneva Convention of 1925. Entry into force: 1928. This document can be viewed online at http://www.fas.harvard.edu/~hsp/1925.html.

The instruments of ratification of and accession to the present Protocol will remain deposited in the archives of the Government of the French Republic.

The present Protocol will come into force for each signatory Power as from the date of deposit of its ratification, and, from that moment, each Power will be bound as regards other Powers which have already deposited their ratifications.

In witness whereof the Plenipotentiaries have signed the present Protocol.

Done at Geneva in a single copy, the seventeenth day of June, One Thousand Nine Hundred and Twenty-Five.

Biological Weapons, Literally Older Than Methuselah[2]

Maybe it started with Moses. The biblical story of Exodus mentions 10 plagues God inflicted on the Egyptians for the Pharaoh's refusal to free the Jews from slavery: blood, frogs, vermin, flies, murrain, boils, hail, locusts, darkness and the slaying of the first-born.

Modern biology, which in the last century has produced almost miraculous cures for some of man's most intractable diseases, now may be harnessed to produce an "Eleventh Plague," an image that Leonard A. Cole, a political scientist, seized on in his book exploring the politics of biological and chemical warfare.

Unlike chemical and even nuclear arms, those other weapons of mass destruction, biological agents are living weapons. And although technology is making the creation of ever more deadly strains possible, the idea of using germs in warfare has a long history.

Though historians and biologists dispute some of the more famous stories linked to biological weapons in war, including some biblical accounts of plagues and pandemics, the list of historical attempts at such use is impressive. Here are a few of the more celebrated cases.

"Medical Management of Biological Casualties," a handbook issued in 1996 by the Army Medical Research Institute of Infectious Diseases at Fort Detrick, Md., says that two of the earliest reported uses of biological weapons in war occurred in the sixth century B.C. when the Assyrians poisoned enemy wells with rye ergot (a fungus disease), and Solon used the purgative herb hellebore during the siege of Krissa.

Fomites, or objects that harbor and can transmit disease, have been used deliberately to transmit disease since antiquity, said another group of scientists from Fort Detrick, writing in an August 1997 issue of the Journal of the American Medical Association.

They say that modern attempts to "weaponize" deadly biological toxins like botulin and ricin were anticipated by

Modern biology, which in the last century has produced almost miraculous cures for some of man's most intractable diseases, now may be harnessed to produce an "Eleventh Plague."

---

2. Article by Judith Miller from the *New York Times* B p7 Sep. 19, 1998. Copyright © 1998 the New York Times Company. Reprinted with permission.

aboriginal South Americans with neolithic technology who used curare and amphibian-derived toxins as arrow poisons.

In 1346, during the siege of Kaffa, now Feodossia in Ukraine, the attacking Tartar army had an epidemic of plague. The scientists argue in the medical association journal that the Tartars, "attempting to convert their misfortune into an opportunity," catapulted the corpses of plague victims over Kaffa's city walls, touching off a plague among the inhabitants that eventually forced them to surrender. Some infected people (and possibly plague-infected rats as well) who left Kaffa, sailing off to Constantinople, Genoa, Venice and other Mediterranean ports, may have contributed to starting the Black Death pandemic that spread through Europe in the 14th and 15th centuries, killing a substantial percentage of the population.

In 1710, Russian troops may also have used what the scientists called the old "plague-infected corpse tactic" against Sweden.

Smallpox has long been a germ of choice among biowarriors. In the 15th century, Pizarro is reported to have presented South American natives with variola-contaminated clothing. The English apparently did the same during the French and Indian War in 1754-67. According to the medical journal article, Sir Jeffrey Amherst, commander of the British forces in North America, suggested that smallpox be used to reduce American Indian tribes hostile to Britain, and on June 24, 1763, Captain Ecuyer, one of Amherst's aides, gave blankets and a handkerchief from the smallpox hospital to the Indians.

"I hope it will have the desired effect," he noted in his journal. It apparently did, though the scientists argue that cause and effect are uncertain since smallpox epidemics had been occurring among Indians for more than 200 years after initial contacts with Europeans.

The 19th-century discoveries of modern microbiology led to technological breakthroughs in biowarfare, especially the ability to isolate and produce stocks of specific pathogens, or deadly germs. World War I provided ample opportunities to use them.

There is substantial evidence, say the scientists in the journal article, that Germany developed an ambitious biological warfare program and that German agents inoculated horses and cattle with glanders in the United States before the animals were shipped to France. The Bucharest Institute of Bacteriology and Pathology identified germ cultures that were confiscated from the German Legation in Romania in 1916 as B. anthracis and B. mallei. And German agents operating allegedly used Burkholderia mallei in Mesopotamia to inoculate 4,500 mules and in France to infect the French cavalry's horses.

The use of chemical and biological weapons in World War I caused public revulsion and helped bring about the 1925 Geneva Protocol, which prohibited the use of germ or chemical weapons in warfare. But the protocol did not ban basic research, production or possession of such agents, and many countries that signed the accord specifically preserved the right to retaliate if they were attacked.

While Germany tried to develop biological weapons in World War II, the only known German use of them then was "the pollution of a reservoir in northwestern Bohemia with sewage in May 1945," according to the Fort Detrick scientists. Japan, however, used a series of germ weapons on a vast scale, especially against prisoners in Manchuria from 1932 until the end of World War II. Thousands of prisoners died after being infected with B. anthracis, meningitidis, shigella and yersinia pestis, to name but a few. Japan also dropped germ-filled bombs, feathers and cotton wadding from its fighter planes, infecting thousands more in at least 11 Chinese cities.

Japan's program was huge, encompassing 150 buildings, 5 satellite camps and more than 3,000 scientists and technicians, according to the Fort Detrick scientists. As many as 15 million plague-infected fleas were released from aircraft during each attack.

Russia and the United States both launched large offensive biological warfare programs in the early 1940's, but Washington, unlike Moscow, unilaterally abandoned all offensive biological and toxin weapon research and production in 1969. By 1972, all stockpiles of biological agents and munitions were destroyed. In 1972, the United States became a party to a treaty outlawing the development, possession and stockpiling of germs and toxins for offensive purposes. But so did Iraq and Russia, both of which continued to produce germs to be turned into weapons until at least 1990.

The use of chemical and biological weapons in World War I caused public revulsion and helped bring about the 1925 Geneva Protocol.

The Weapon Too Terrible for the Parade of Horribles[3]

Paris—The old enemy from Central Casting has returned to the American stage: Saddam Hussein with his grotesque personality cult, his history of using chemical weapons against his own people and the Iranians, his invasion of Kuwait and his cynical cruelty.

But in mobilizing to bomb him, President Clinton has repeatedly singled out one specific threat: that of the biological weapons that Saddam possesses and appears to be concealing from United Nations inspectors.

This biological threat, of course, has immense psychological impact, conjuring up such staples of the collective sub-conscience as plague and pestilence. Silent, unlike a gun or a bomb, and relatively slow to kill, the germ-as-weapon-of-war terrifies. When Clinton talks of the horrors of biological warfare and the danger that "our children" be exposed to it, he knows he is wielding a potent propaganda weapon.

But how real is the threat from Saddam? Or, perhaps, from one of his agents, slipping quietly into the New York City subway system carrying a flask of lethal anthrax bacteria developed in a makeshift laboratory from a formula so widely available it is on the Internet?

U.N. inspectors have established that Iraq has been engaged in a biological-weapons program for at least 20 years, that in the past it has put anthrax spores into bombs and Scud warheads, and that it has also prepared another lethal substance called Botulinium toxin.

In theory, one gram of anthrax bacteria alone could kill 10 million people. But how much of Iraq's biological arsenal has already been destroyed, and the precise whereabouts of what is left, remains as mysterious as Saddam's ultimate intentions. For the Iraqi leader is operating in what amounts to uncharted territory.

Biological weapons have been made for decades and the idea of using disease to kill or harm an enemy has existed for centuries. The Tartars catapulted plague-infested bodies into the besieged Crimean city of Kaffa in 1346.

---

3. Article by Roger Cohen from the *New York Times* IV p.1 + Feb. 8, 1998. Copyright © 1998 the New York Times Company. Reprinted with permission.

Yet despite Japanese and British experiments during World War II, and elaborate postwar biological-weapons programs in the United States and the Soviet Union, there is no record of their use on any significant scale in recent history.

Therein, of course, lies part of the threat's potency: its mystery. "There's a huge amount of uncertainty because we have not experienced this before," said Dr. Matthew S. Meselson, a Harvard biologist. What is clear, however, is that, while cheap and relatively easy to produce, biological weapons have immense practical drawbacks: they are difficult to deploy effectively, susceptible to the whims of the wind, totally undiscriminating and potentially dangerous to the power or person using them.

A Scud warhead packed with anthrax bacteria will not bother anyone if it explodes at an altitude of 1,000 feet or embeds itself in the ground. The germs have to be at nose level.

When President Richard M. Nixon renounced America's biological-weapons research in 1969, he certainly had pragmatic as well as moral considerations in mind.

But, in the end, it is a unique ethical repugnance, rather than the practical difficulties, that appears to lie behind the shunning of biological weapons.

It is a unique ethical repugnance, rather than the practical difficulties, that appears to lie behind the shunning of biological weapons.

To employ such weapons is, after all, to invoke the enemies of mankind, the bugs on the prowl looking for meat to eat, the vermin always lurking, the rats of the bubonic plague that killed a third of Europe's population in the 14th century—the very natural scourges that medicine has long struggled to control or overcome.

"I do see a distinction between biological weapons and everything else," said Joshua Lederberg, president emeritus at Rockefeller University. "Chemicals don't multiply or proliferate. But biological weapons use active enemies of humanity, the agents that seek our flesh."

Other factors also contribute to what seems to amount to a unique moral anathema: the potentially suicidal aspect of willfully unleashing disease that could come back to infect its purveyor; the blurring of lines between peace and war that accompanies the soundless release into the air of germs, and the instinctive, overwhelming sense shared by most of mankind that disease and poison are afflictions rather than weapons.

Saddam, who showed no reluctance to poison the environment itself when he dumped oil into the Persian Gulf and set

Kuwait's oilfields aflame in 1991, is clearly viewed as particularly menacing because the world stands on the eve of an explosive development of biotechnologies whose benefits could be perverted for sinister use. In this sense, he represents at a crude level a phenomenon that could become much more sophisticated and malevolent.

"All major human advances—the use of stone, of metal, of electronics—have been susceptible to creative and destructive use," said Meselson. "It is the same with biotechnology. We could, in the next century, have biological weapons that manipulate life processes, influence thought patterns, or produce people with extra limbs."

closing

Such scenarios are terrifying. But the very psychological potency of biological weapons may blur a cool assessment of the real threat they contain. Some scientists are troubled by the notion that these weapons constitute some special category of their own, and by the obvious ease with which their ghoulish horror can be manipulated.

"They scare people but they're ineffective as weapons, and that is a major reason why they have not been used," said Dr. Norton Zindler, a biologist at Rockefeller University. "Part of the story today is building Saddam as a villain and a scary guy because he has these biological weapons. But fundamentally, for me, there can be no moral distinction between biological and nuclear weapons. Killing people is killing people."

In France, Italy and the rest of continental Europe, the conviction is fairly widespread that America is deliberately exaggerating the threat of Saddam's biological and chemical weapons in order to justify an attack.

Recent unrelated events—including last week's ski-lift accident in Italy, caused by a low-flying American military plane, and the deeply unsettling execution in Texas of Karla Faye Tucker—have stirred a wave of anti-American sentiment based on the idea of a "Yankee" culture run amok.

In one opinion article in the Italian newspaper *La Repubblica*, the author Giorgio Bocca drew a link between the Italian accident, American movies that are "little other than an apology for military cretinism" and the looming attack on Iraq, planned "without consulting America's allies or those who live there."

Clinton will have to reckon, at least peripherally, with these European sentiments if he does decide to bomb. But it is already clear that he and the Pentagon regard Iraq as a special case, and that biological weapons are only part of the story.

The most intense recent bout of killing in the world, in Rwanda, was largely perpetrated with very old instruments of war: knives and machetes. And nuclear weapons, which themselves added a whole new meaning to weapons of indiscriminate destruction, have proliferated with what has amounted, in several instances, to a tacit U.S. acquiescence.

Whatever the real importance of U.S. concerns about biological weaponry, in a way Clinton has already trumped Saddam. By painting Saddam as the agent who could unleash such warfare on the world, the Americans have been using the threat rather effectively in recent days to build a case for attacking him with more conventional ordinance.

In addition to moral outrage, after all, the confrontation with Iraq is a head-on collision of major U.S. interests with a particularly murderous dictator.

Beyond the destruction of chemical and biological weapons, an eventual bombing campaign would serve several long-term U.S. interests in the region: the maintenance of a weak Iraq, but one not so weak that it will disintegrate; the reinforcement of the conservative gulf regimes and cheap supplies of oil; the maintenance of a rough balance of power between Iraq and Iran.

"Sometimes you have to act just to maintain the status quo," said Jonathan Eyal, the director of studies at the Royal Institute of Strategic Studies in London. "You need an aggressive policy to maintain a defensive one. It may not sound that glorious, and it's much less exciting than the talk of biological weapons, but it's critically important."

II. The Persian Gulf and Iraq

Editor's Introduction

Perhaps the single issue that has brought chemical and biological warfare to the forefront of world affairs in recent years has been the weapons stockpiles that the nation of Iraq is suspected of possessing. It is known that Iraqi dictator Saddam Hussein ordered the use of poisonous gas during the Iran-Iraq War of 1980–1988, and that chemical agents were also used by Hussein to quell uprisings among his own people. Following the Persian Gulf Conflict in 1991, the United Nations has attempted to keep a close watch on Iraq to prevent the buildup of chemical or biological weapons and to ferret out whatever weapons may already exist. To what degree such an arsenal exists today is still unclear, however the fact remains that Hussein has proved highly uncooperative with the United Nations, repeatedly refusing to grant permission for UN inspectors to enter sites they suspect of containing prohibited substances or devices. Adding to suspicions directed toward Hussein is the unresolved issue of what has become known as "Gulf War syndrome," a mysterious malady reported by American veterans of the Gulf conflict which many attribute to exposure to dangerous chemicals in Iraq.

The first article in this chapter, "Hide and Seek," comes from the *New Republic.* In it, W. Seth Carus recaps the dilemma faced by the United Nations Special Commission (UNSCOM) assigned to inspect Iraqi facilities for chemical and biological weapons and to eliminate whatever illegal weapons are discovered. Concerns over what Hussein may be hiding—including a vast supply of the deadly toxin VX—are explored. Carus also addresses what has been done about Iraq's sizeable biological weapons program, which was exposed in 1995.

"Anthrax for Export," by William Blum, which appeared in the *Progressive,* deals with the controversial issue of American aid to Hussein during the 1980s. According to Blum's piece, raw materials provided by the U.S. were used by Iraq to develop biological and chemical weapons for use against Iran. The author lists some of the chemical and biological compounds reportedly exported to Iraq, as well as some of the American corporations known to have supplied those compounds. In fairness, Blum acknowledges some of the justifications made by a number of the listed corporations, in which they point out that they had no knowledge of Iraq's intentions. A number of congressional investigations into these unfortunate dealings are also described.

The next item is of particular note because it is an interview with one of the U.N. inspectors actually assigned to the Persian Gulf. In "Unearthing Weapons of Mass Destruction," UNSCOM official Terrence Taylor relates to Darius Bazargan of *The Middle East* his firsthand experiences dealing with Iraq. Taylor firmly believes that Hussein possesses a great deal more than he has already admitted, and provides past examples as evidence. He is also opposed to the loosening of UN sanctions against Iraq, saying that Hussein is capitalizing on divisions among the UN members to take some of the pressure off his own nation.

In "How Iraq's Biological Weapons Program Came to Light," William J. Broad and Judith Miller of the *New York Times* extensively review the chain of events surrounding one of UNSCOM's most important discoveries. In 1995, UN inspectors learned that Iraq had acquired nutrients that could be used for growing deadly germs. Saddam Hussein's son-in-law Lt. Gen. Hussein Kamal, who soon thereafter defected to Jordan, confirmed the suspicions of the inspectors. In addition to summarizing these events, the article gives a rundown of Iraq's chemical and biological warfare experiments over the past several decades, and takes an in-depth look at the efforts that went into uncovering crucial information about Iraq's capabilities.

The last piece in this chapter focuses on Gulf War syndrome, which has become a major topic of debate over the past decade. In "Secret Casualties of the Gulf," which first appeared in *American Legion* magazine, Joe Stuteville talks to former CIA analysts Patrick and Robin Eddington, who claim they have evidence that not only were American troops exposed to poisonous chemicals during the Persian Gulf War, but that the exposure was the result of direct Iraqi attacks. Stuteville chronicles the efforts of the Eddingtons to make their findings public, in the face of what the former analysts describe as a government cover-up.

Hide and Seek[1]

Saddam Hussein is at it again. Last week, the Iraqi dictator banned American inspectors working for the United Nations from investigating Iraq's development of weapons of mass destruction. Then he threatened to shoot down U.S. spy planes flying over its territory. Washington quickly denounced Saddam, but, in all the outcry, no one answered the critical question: What is the Iraqi dictator so determined to hide?

Though the United Nations Special Commission (UNSCOM) has been able to locate and destroy Iraq's stock of chemical weapons and the manufacturing facilities to replenish it, there are still major gaps in our knowledge of Iraq's chemical weapons capabilities. The Iraqis, for instance, have admitted that they filled as many as 75 Scud missile warheads with nerve agents, but only 30 of these warheads were ever examined by UNSCOM and destroyed.

Then there is Iraq's secret program to produce VX—the most toxic chemical agent in the world. Recent probing by U.N. inspectors uncovered a far more advanced VX effort than Western officials suspected. Earlier this year, the Iraqis finally conceded that they had produced small quantities of VX, although UNSCOM suspects that it might have made far larger quantities.

Biological weapons are another concern. For years, Iraq denied that it had an offensive biological weapons program, insisting it was merely "researching" such agents as anthrax and botulinum toxin. The Iraqis stuck to this story for so long that even some U.N. inspectors began to believe it. In the summer of 1995, only one issue kept UNSCOM from officially approving the lifting of sanctions against Iraq: Baghdad's acquisition of a substantial amount of growth media—a substance that can be used to produce deadly biological agents. The Iraqis claimed it was for peaceful purposes, but could not explain where it was all used.

The myth that Iraq had only a minor biological weapons program was completely shattered in August 1995, when Saddam's son-in-law, Hussein Kamal, who had been responsible for many of Iraq's special weapons programs, defected

1. Article by W. Seth Carus for the *New Republic* p28 Nov. 24, 1997. Copyright © 1997 the *New Republic*. Reprinted by permission. W. Seth Carus is a defense analyst at the Center for Counterproliferation Research at the National Defense University.

Only the constant monitoring efforts of UNSCOM prevent Iraq from once again having the ability to wage biological warfare.

to Jordan. The U.N. soon discovered just how little it really knew about what Iraq had been up to. In addition to the agents identified in 1991, U.N. officials discovered that Iraq was working on a host of other agents. It had produced ricin toxin in small quantities. Moreover, its scientists had researched several viral diseases, including hemorrhagic conjunctivitis, rotavirus, and camel pox. And it had explored agents that could be used against economic targets, including fungus to attack wheat crops.

Iraq also confessed to creating—and field testing—an arsenal of biological weapons. According to Iraqi reports, Saddam's officers filled 166 aircraft bombs (100 with botulinum toxin, 50 with anthrax, and 16 with aflatoxin) and 25 Al-Husayn missile warheads (13 with botulinum toxin, ten with aflatoxin, and two with anthrax).

As a result of these revelations, UNSCOM conducted additional inspections that have uncovered even more information; and it forced Iraq to destroy certain facilities that the U.N. inspectors had earlier allowed the Iraqis to keep, including the single-cell protein facility at Al Hakam, which had been used to produce massive quantities of anthrax and botulinum toxin.

In September, the Iraqis finally gave UNSCOM a 700-page report that once again was to provide a "full, final and complete disclosure" of its biological weapons program. But a review by UNSCOM of this latest report suggested that it was "incomplete and contained significant inaccuracies." Experts who follow Iraq's biological weapons program believe that stocks of biological agents are still being hidden, and that, if need be, Iraq could produce biological weapons in a matter of months. Indeed, only the constant monitoring efforts of UNSCOM prevent Iraq from once again having the ability to wage biological warfare.

The same is true of Iraqi missile capabilities. Though UNSCOM believes, after intensive investigation, that it has accounted for all of Iraq's Scuds, it is less certain about all the Iraqi-produced components. And Iraq continues to work on shorter range missiles permitted by the U.N., including an effort to develop new guided missiles with ranges of 100 to 150 kilometers. Some analysts believe that Iraq retains a capability to produce missiles with ranges even greater than 150 kilometers. Indeed, only last year, inspectors discovered that the Iraqis were acquiring guidance systems from dismantled Soviet intercontinental ballistic missiles.

These could, along with other long-range missiles, deliver nuclear weapons. In its most recent report to the Security Council, the International Atomic Energy Agency essentially concluded that it could make no additional progress in figuring out what happened to Iraq's former nuclear programs. As a result, it has decided to terminate its efforts without closing the case on Iraq's past activity. Significantly, some members of the Security Council, especially France and Russia, have used the IAEA report to claim that Iraq has made progress in meeting U.N. requirements, thus justifying a relaxation of sanctions.

Yet this seems dangerously premature. The hardest part of making a nuclear weapon is obtaining the fissile material for it. Iraq spent billions of dollars on its nuclear weapons program, primarily to develop and build an infrastructure for producing the fissile material essential for atomic bombs.

In particular, the Iraqis were developing several methods for producing highly enriched uranium. Iraq also wanted to produce plutonium, and had begun a program to replace the Osirak reactor destroyed by the Israelis in 1981. But no evidence was ever found that Baghdad had actually begun construction of a new reactor. So it will likely take Iraq years to rebuild the infrastructure needed to produce its own fissile material.

The problem, however, is that Iraq had a viable nuclear weapon design, and if Saddam purchases highly enriched uranium through illicit channels, Iraq could build a nuclear weapon in a relatively short period of time. The Iraqis are known to have good contacts in the former Soviet Union, and Russian sources might be willing to supply Iraq with highly enriched uranium.

All of this helps explain why Iraq is so determined to keep out American inspectors. It also explains why Iraq has been willing to forsake more than $100 billion in oil revenue rather than come clean with the U.N. Saddam clearly believes that, if he succeeds, the cost will be much higher to the rest of the world—and, at least on this point, he may be right.

Anthrax for Export[2]

The United States almost went to war against Iraq in February because of Saddam Hussein's weapons program. In his State of the Union address, President Clinton castigated Hussein for "developing nuclear, chemical, and biological weapons and the missiles to deliver them."

"You cannot defy the will of the world," the President proclaimed. "You have used weapons of mass destruction before. We are determined to deny you the capacity to use them again."

Most Americans listening to the President did not know that the United States supplied Iraq with much of the raw material for creating a chemical and biological warfare program. Nor did the media report that U.S. companies sold Iraq more than $1 billion worth of the components needed to build nuclear weapons and diverse types of missiles, including the infamous Scud.

When Iraq engaged in chemical and biological warfare in the 1980s, barely a peep of moral outrage could be heard from Washington, as it kept supplying Saddam with the materials he needed to build weapons.

From 1980 to 1988, Iraq and Iran waged a terrible war against each other, a war that might not have begun if President Jimmy Carter had not given the Iraqis a green light to attack Iran, in response to repeated provocations. Throughout much of the war, the United States provided military aid and intelligence information to both sides, hoping that each would inflict severe damage on the other.

Noam Chomsky suggests that this strategy is a way for America to keep control of its oil supply:

"It's been a leading, driving doctrine of U.S. foreign policy since the 1940s that the vast and unparalleled energy resources of the Gulf region will be effectively dominated by the United States and its clients, and, crucially, that no independent indigenous force will be permitted to have a substantial influence on the administration of oil production and price."

During the Iran-Iraq war, Iraq received the lion's share of American support because at the time Iran was regarded as the greater threat to U.S. interests. According to a 1994 Sen-

The United States supplied Iraq with much of the raw material for creating a chemical and biological warfare program.

---

2. Article by William Blum for the *Progressive* p18-20 Apr. 1998. Copyright © 1998 the *Progressive*. Reprinted with permission.

ate report, private American suppliers, licensed by the U.S. Department of Commerce, exported a witch's brew of biological and chemical materials to Iraq from 1985 through 1989. Among the biological materials, which often produce slow, agonizing death, were:

- Bacillus Anthracis, cause of anthrax.
- Clostridium Botulinum, a source of botulinum toxin.
- Histoplasma Capsulatam, cause of a disease attacking lungs, brain, spinal cord, and heart.
- Brucella Melitensis, a bacteria that can damage major organs.
- Clostridium Perfringens, a highly toxic bacteria causing systemic illness.
- Clostridium tetani, a highly toxigenic substance.

Also on the list: Escherichia coli (E. coli), genetic materials, human and bacterial DNA, and dozens of other pathogenic biological agents. "These biological materials were not attenuated or weakened and were capable of reproduction," the Senate report stated. "It was later learned that these microorganisms exported by the United States were identical to those the United Nations inspectors found and removed from the Iraqi biological warfare program."

The report noted further that U.S. exports to Iraq included the precursors to chemical-warfare agents, plans for chemical and biological warfare production facilities, and chemical-warhead filling equipment.

The exports continued to at least November 28, 1989, despite evidence that Iraq was engaging in chemical and biological warfare against Iranians and Kurds since as early as 1984.

The American company that provided the most biological materials to Iraq in the 1980s was American Type Culture Collection of Maryland and Virginia, which made seventy shipments of the anthrax-causing germ and other pathogenic agents, according to a 1996 *Newsday* story.

Other American companies also provided Iraq with the chemical or biological compounds, or the facilities and equipment used to create the compounds for chemical and biological warfare. Among these suppliers were the following:

- Alcolac International, a Baltimore chemical manufacturer already linked to the illegal shipment of chemicals to Iran, shipped large quantities of thiodiglycol (used to make mustard gas) as well as other chemical and biological ingredients, according to a 1989 story in the *New*

York Times.

- Nu Kraft Mercantile Corp. of Brooklyn (affiliated with the United Steel and Strip Corporation) also supplied Iraq with huge amounts of thiodiglycol, the *Times* reported.
- Celery Corp., Charlotte, NC
- Matrix-Churchill Corp., Cleveland, OH (regarded as a front for the Iraqi government, according to Representative Henry Gonzalez, Democrat of Texas, who quoted U.S. intelligence documents to this effect in a 1992 speech on the House floor).

The following companies were also named as chemical and biological materials suppliers in the 1992 Senate hearings on "United States export policy toward Iraq prior to Iraq's invasion of Kuwait":

- Mouse Master, Lilburn, GA
- Sullaire Corp., Charlotte, NC
- Pure Aire, Charlotte, NC
- Posi Seal, Inc., N. Stonington, CT
- Union Carbide, Danbury, CT
- Evapco, Taneytown, MD
- Gorman-Rupp, Mansfield, OH

Additionally, several other companies were sued in connection with their activities providing Iraq with chemical or biological supplies: subsidiaries or branches of Fisher Controls International, Inc., St. Louis; Rhone-Poulenc, Inc., Princeton, NJ; Bechtel Group, Inc., San Francisco; and Lummus Crest, Inc., Bloomfield, NJ, which built one chemical plant in Iraq and, before the Iraqi invasion of Kuwait in August 1990, was building an ethylene facility. Ethylene is a necessary ingredient for thiodiglycol.

In 1994, a group of twenty-six veterans, suffering from what has come to be known as Gulf War Syndrome, filed a billion-dollar lawsuit in Houston against Fisher, Rhone-Poulenc, Bechtel Group, and Lummus Crest, as well as American Type Culture Collection (ATCC) and six other firms, for helping Iraq to obtain or produce the compounds which the veterans blamed for their illnesses. By 1998, the number of plaintiffs has risen to more than 4,000 and the suit is still pending in Texas.

A Pentagon study in 1994 dismissed links between chemical and biological weapons and Gulf War Syndrome. *Newsday* later disclosed, however, that the man who headed the study, Nobel laureate Joshua Lederberg, was a director of ATCC. Moreover, at the time of ATCC's shipments to Iraq, which the Commerce Department approved, the firm's CEO was a member of the Commerce Department's Technical Advisory Committee, the paper found.

A larger number of American firms supplied Iraq with the specialized computers, lasers, testing and analyzing equipment, and other instruments and hardware vital to the manufacture of nuclear weapons, missiles, and delivery systems. Computers, in particular, play a key role in nuclear weapons development. Advanced computers make it feasible to avoid carrying out nuclear test explosions, thus preserving the program's secrecy. The 1992 Senate hearings implicated the following firms:

- Kennametal, Latrobe, PA
- Hewlett Packard, Palo Alto, CA
- International Computer Systems, CA, SC, and TX
- Perkins-Elmer, Norwalk, CT
- BDM Corp., McLean, VA
- Leybold Vacuum Systems, Export, PA
- Spectra Physics, Mountain View, CA
- Unisys Corp., Blue Bell, PA
- Finnigan MAT, San Jose, Ca
- Scientific Atlanta, Atlanta, GA
- Spectral Data Corp., Champaign, IL
- Tektronix, Wilsonville, OR
- Veeco Instruments, Inc., Plainview, NY
- Wiltron Company, Morgan Hill, CA

Some of the companies said later that they had no idea Iraq might ever put their products to military use.

The House report also singled out: TI Coating, Inc., Axel Electronics, Data General Corp., Gerber Systems, Honeywell, Inc., Digital Equipment Corp., Sackman Associates, Rockwell Collins International, Wild Magnavox Satellite Survey, Zeta Laboratories, Carl Schenck, EZ Logic Data, International Imaging Systems, Semetex Corp., and Thermo Jarrell Ash Corporation.

Some of the companies said later that they had no idea Iraq might ever put their products to military use. A spokesperson for Hewlett Packard said the company believed that the Iraqi recipient of its shipments, Saad 16, was an institution of higher learning. In fact, in 1990 the *Wall Street Journal* described Saad 16 as "a heavily fortified, state-of-the-art complex for aircraft construction, missile design, and, almost certainly, nuclear-weapons research."

Other corporations recognized the military potential of their goods but considered it the government's job to worry about it. "Every once in a while you kind of wonder when you sell something to a certain country," said Robert Finney, president of Electronic Associates, Inc., which supplied Saad

16 with a powerful computer that could be used for missile testing and development. "But it's not up to us to make foreign policy," Finney told the *Wall Street Journal.*

In 1982, the Reagan Administration took Iraq off its list of countries alleged to sponsor terrorism, making it eligible to receive high-tech items generally denied to those on the list. Conventional military sales began in December of that year. Representative Samuel Gejdenson, Democrat of Connecticut, chairman of a House subcommittee investigating "United States Exports of Sensitive Technology to Iraq," stated in 1991:

"From 1985 to 1990, the United States Government approved 771 licenses for the export to Iraq of $1.5 billion worth of biological agents and high-tech equipment with military application. [Only thirty-nine applications were rejected.] The United States spent virtually an entire decade making sure that Saddam Hussein had almost whatever he wanted.... The Administration has never acknowledged that it took this course of action, nor has it explained why it did so. In reviewing documents and press accounts, and interviewing knowledgeable sources, it becomes clear that United States export-control policy was directed by U.S. foreign policy as formulated by the State Department, and it was U.S. foreign policy to assist the regime of Saddam Hussein."

Subsequently, Representative John Dingell, Democrat of Michigan, investigated the Department of Energy concerning an unheeded 1989 warning about Iraq's nuclear weapons program. In 1992, he accused the DOE of punishing employees who raised the alarm and rewarding those who didn't take it seriously. One DOE scientist, interviewed by Dingell's Energy and Commerce Committee, was especially conscientious about the mission of the nuclear non-proliferation program. For his efforts, he received very little cooperation, inadequate staff, and was finally forced to quit in frustration. "It was impossible to do a good job," said William Emel. His immediate manager, who tried to get the proliferation program fully staffed, was chastened by management and removed from his position. Emel was hounded by the DOE at his new job as well.

Another Senate committee, investigating "United States export policy toward Iraq prior to Iraq's invasion of Kuwait," heard testimony in 1992 that Commerce Department personnel "changed information on sixty-eight licenses; that references to military end uses were deleted and the designation 'military truck' was changed. This was done on licenses having a total value of over $1 billion." Testimony made clear that the White House was "involved" in "a deliberate effort ... to alter these documents and mislead the Congress."

American foreign-policy makers maintained a cooperative relationship with U.S. corporate interests in the region. In 1985, Marshall Wiley, former U.S. ambassador to Oman, set up the Washington-based U.S.-Iraq Business Forum, which lobbied in Washington on behalf of Iraq to promote U.S. trade with that country. Speaking of the Forum's creation, Wiley later explained, "I went to the State Department and told them what I was planning to do, and they said, 'Fine. It sounds like a good idea.' It was our policy to increase exports to Iraq."

Though the government readily approved most sales to Iraq, officials at Defense and Commerce clashed over some of them (with the State Department and the White House backing Commerce).

"If an item was in dispute, my attitude was if they were readily available from other markets, I didn't see why we should deprive American markets," explained Richard Murphy in 1990. Murphy was Assistant Secretary of State for Near Eastern and South Asian Affairs from 1983 to 1989.

As it turned out, Iraq did not use any chemical or biological weapons against U.S. forces in the Gulf War. But American planes bombed chemical and biological weapons storage facilities with abandon, potentially dooming tens of thousands of American soldiers to lives of prolonged and permanent agony, and an unknown number of Iraqis to a similar fate. Among the symptoms reported by the affected soldiers are memory loss, scarred lungs, chronic fatigue, severe headache, raspy voice, and passing out. The Pentagon estimates that nearly 100,000 American soldiers were exposed to sarin gas alone.

After the war, White House and Defense Department officials tried their best to deny that Gulf War Syndrome had anything to do with the bombings. The suffering of soldiers was not their overriding concern. The top concerns of the Bush and Clinton Administrations were to protect perceived U.S. interests in the Middle East, and to ensure that American corporations still had healthy balance sheets.

The Pentagon estimates that nearly 100,000 American soldiers were exposed to sarin gas alone.

Unearthing Weapons of Mass Destruction[3]

Terrence Taylor, UNSCOM inspector for biological weapons, recently returned from Iraq. Here he tells Darius Bazargan about his work for the UN and his fears about continuing Iraqi evasion as Baghdad secretly adds germ warfare to its arsenal of Weapons of Mass Destruction (WMD).

Darius Bazargan: Some members of the UN Security Council (UNSC) are starting to waver over keeping sanctions on Iraq. Has that affected your work?

Terrence Taylor: Yes, that's already happening. Within his latest report Rolf Ekeus (the last head of UNSCOM) complains about the lack of Iraqi cooperation with the long-term monitoring programme. The Iraqis are doing this because they know that there are squabbles among members of the Security Council and they are exploiting that as far as they can. It is our intrusive inspections that are a major element in maintaining the consensus of the Security Council. We are able to produce evidence every time to show the Iraqis haven't told us everything. This is how it goes on, we find it out and then they declare it. Now, after my latest mission they will say "Oh yes, we did do this work on this particular agent."

The commission has this tough job of uncovering the evidence which then forces Iraq to make a declaration. The Iraqi policy seems to be that they tell the world only what we already know.

DB: What is to stop the Iraqis from hiding evidence once they know where you are going on an inspection?

TT: The Special Commission is not required to give any notice about where we are going. It begins like this: I sit in our base at the Canal Hotel in downtown Baghdad and then just drive out of the gates with my team. The Iraqi escort teams are waiting and they follow me. I don't say a thing. They are riding along with their outriders and you have this extraordinary scene like something out of the Keystone Cops going down the road and they're all wondering where you are going. They always ask me: "Where are you going tomor-

---

3. Interview by Darius Bazargan. From *The Midle East* p 14-15 July / Aug. 1997. Copyright © 1997 the Middle East/I.C. Publications Ltd. Reprinted with permission.

row?" and I say "I don't know. I'll tell you at 9 o'clock tomorrow morning."

DB: How did you come to find evidence that Iraq had biological weapons?

TT: Because they said "We have no biological weapons programme" the Commission said "Right, we must list every site that has a dual purpose capability, anywhere that could be involved in the development and production of biological weapons." That included buildings ranging from university colleges, like the College of Pharmacology, the Department of Hydrobiology, hospitals, anything that has fermentation processes like breweries, or dairies through to pharmaceutical production plants and veterinary vaccine production plants.

I'm not naming them all but we listed over 80 sites. We had to work our way through all these and in doing that we uncovered other bits of evidence. Probably one of the most significant ones was in March 1995 when we found evidence of the importation of growth media, a substance in which you can culture pathogenic organisms. They are used in hospitals, but in tiny quantities. We found that Iraq was importing tons of the stuff, we had evidence of 40 tons. That would be enough to keep the country going for a decade, so clearly this was being used for some other purpose.

We uncovered this evidence in several ways; for example from companies who'd exported the stuff, we got the conveyencing receipts—the documentation from those companies and went to the Iraqi authorities and said: "Look, you've imported 40 tons, where is it?" They scratched their heads for a while and tried to come up with a story. "Yes, it all went to hospitals, first through our medical stores system and then out to regional hospitals," they told us.

We said "Fine, okay, give us the docments that show us where."

"Well," they said, "some of it was destroyed in riots, there was rioting in the provinces." That was meant to account for about 10 tons of it, so we said: "Okay, where is the rest?"

They produced a whole series of documents and I had to go and find out if they were genuine or false. Most of them were plainly false. The Iraqis were forced to admit, "Yes, well, we did have a weapons programme but we weren't weaponising it." They didn't admit it straight away, of course.

DB: What is the difference between having a weapons programme and "weaponising" something?

TT: It's bad enough to produce the agents for weapons, that would be illegal under the Biological Weapons Convention. The next step is a major one, where you design the delivery means, the delivery systems. The engineering to disperse biological weapons is not something you can just go and do, you can't just stuff it into an agricultural sprayer. You have to get things right.

They've used artillery shells, 122mm rockets, air-delivered bombs called R-400s which they modified especially and they were working on prototype spray-tanks for aircraft. Fortunately, at the time of the Gulf War they had difficulty with the spray nozzles of the devices and had not quite completed work on them.

And they were widening the range of agents all the time. Noone who knows anything about biological weapons was surprised by the range of agents they used and were working on.

They had bacteria, viruses, toxins—the whole range. Some incapacitating, some lethal, like anthrax, not botulinum and other very nasty weapons such as a toxin called Aflatoxin which incapacitates people and is highly carcinogenic and kills you in a very nasty way. Things like clostridium perphlingum, which causes a nasty effect called gas gangrene which causes your flesh to rot. They were even dexperimenting with things like camel-pox and animal diseases to see what their effects might be and if they could be weaponised. Also things like wheat cover-smut which is an anti-crop agent. It was an amazing range of a programme which quite a lot of effort was put into, and it was interesting that the person who was responsible for production said that they accelerated the rate of production of biological weapon agents after the invasion of Kuwait and before Desert Shield.

DB: What did you discover on this latest trip?

TT: I can't give the details, but we found evidence of another biological agent, a toxin. They had mentioned it before, but the work was far more extensive than had been declared. What they want to attain is the capability, because you don't need to actually store the agent. What you need is the capability to produce the agent at short notice.

DB: Are you worried that they may have kept something really serious back?

TT: Yes, a lot of other people are too, not just me. Rolf Ekeus says they are re-hiding missiles. I mean, here we are with the most intrusive inspection regime that any state has ever experienced, an international inspection regime, and they can still hide big things like Scud missiles.

DB: In the long-term, imagine the day comes when you feel UNSCOM can give Iraq a clean bill of health and it gets one. Realistically, surely as soon as they have got that, Iraq is just going to start building WMDs again.

TT: If it is still this regime then, yes. That's my personal view and I think that is the US government's view too. This regime is never going to get a clean bill of health. Well, I wouldn't go so far as to say that, but as long as you have the present regime in place it's hard to imagine they would quit, given the extraordinary efforts they have taken to hide things from the Commission.

DB: But looking at the military policies of neighbouring states, one would assume that any Iraqi government would want to have equivalent WMD capabilities, the same as everyone around them.

TT: There is certainly a lot of substance to that argument. But I think I would want to make that judgement only when I found out who was in power and what their relations might be with the Western powers and with the US in particular. But you raise a very important question. If Saddam Hussein were to die, for example, and not necessarily be pushed out by a coup, what would follow?

The great fear is that Iraq would become an Islamic state. But whoever is in power in Iraq has obligations to UNSC Resolution 687 not to have any WMDs, including missiles of more than 150km range, and to make complete declarations about that. Also there are issues of human rights, regardless of who is in power, and reparations and return of prisoners. That's all to do with Iraq, not a given government. They must also accept UNSC Resolution 715, the long-term compliance monitoring. They must accept the inspection regime, no matter who is in power, so this will continue.

Here we are with the most intrusive inspection regime that any state has ever experienced . . . and they can still hide big things like Scud missiles.

How Iraq's Biological Weapons Program Came to Light[4]

On a January day in 1995, Dr. Rod Barton, a United Nations weapons inspector with a gambler's instinct, decided to try bluffing the Iraqis. Ever since their defeat in the Persian Gulf war, they had steadfastly denied ever making any kind of germ weapons, despite much evidence to the contrary.

Barton, a 46-year-old Australian biologist, did not have much in his hand—just two pieces of paper. The documents proved nothing but were provocative: They showed that in the 1980s, Iraq had bought about 10 tons of nutrients for growing germs, far more than needed for civilian work, from a British company.

[Iraq] had made enough deadly microbes to kill all the people on earth several times over.

"That was all I had," Barton recalled in an interview. "Not a full house, just two deuces. So I played them both."

Sitting across from four Iraqi generals and scientists in a windowless room near the University of Baghdad, Barton laid the documents on the table. Did these, he asked, help refresh the Iraqis' memories?

"They went ashen," he recalled.

That meeting marked a turning point. In the months that followed, Iraq dropped its denials and grudgingly admitted that it had run an elaborate program to produce germ weapons, eventually confessing that it had made enough deadly microbes to kill all the people on earth several times over.

U.N. officials say these disclosures are still seriously incomplete, as does Washington, which has come to the brink of military conflict with Baghdad over the issue.

The U.N. inspectors are now poised to return to Iraq under an accord in which Iraq has promised full cooperation. But the story of the seven-year hunt for secret biological weapons, as recounted by U.S., U.N. and private experts, suggests that the inspectors may have a rocky time. It also shows why they believe that Baghdad is still hiding missiles and germ weapons, and the means to make both.

Among the disclosures were these:

- Just before the gulf war in 1991, Iraqi President Saddam Hussein's son-in-law began a crash military program

---

4. Article by William J. Broad and Judith Miller for the *New York Times* Feb. 26, 1998. Copyright © 1998 the New York Times Company. Reprinted with permission.

intended to give Iraq the ability to wipe out Israel's population with germ weapons, an Iraqi general told inspectors. MiG fighters, each carrying 250 gallons of microbes, were to be flown by remote control to release anthrax over Israel. One pilotless plane was flight-tested with simulated germs just before the war began, but the attack was never attempted.

- The locations of more than 150 bombs and warheads built by the Iraqis to dispense germs are a mystery, as are the whereabouts of a dozen special nozzles that Iraq fashioned in the 1980s to spray germs from helicopters and aircraft.
- On nearly all recent missions, inspectors have found undeclared "dual use" items like germ nutrients, growth tanks and concentrators, all of which have legitimate uses but can also make deadly pathogens for biological warfare.

Today, despite progress in penetrating Iraqi secrecy, inspectors say they remain uncertain about most of Saddam's facilities to wage biological warfare.

The inspectors have found traces of military germs and their seed stocks but none of the thousands of gallons of biological agents that the Iraqis made before the 1991 gulf war. Baghdad says it destroyed the older material but offers no proof.

And the inspectors are unsure of the extent to which Iraq has solved the technical challenges of delivering germs to targets—a problem that bedeviled other states experimenting with biological arms.

Finally, the U.N. inspectors have suspicions—but no proof—that Baghdad is hiding germs and delivery systems. Their worries are based, in part, on a chilling calculus of missing weapons: The United Nations can account for only 25 of the 157 germ bombs that Iraq has acknowledged making for its air force.

And inspectors have no idea of the whereabouts of some 25 germ warheads made for missiles with a range of 400 miles; Baghdad says it destroyed them but, again, offers no proof.

Richard Butler, chairman of the U.N. Special Commission charged with eliminating such weapons, said in report after report that the uncertainties are disturbing and legion. He recently told the Security Council that the 639-page document that comprises Iraq's latest "full, final and complete" declaration, its fifth to date, "fails to give a remotely credible account" of Baghdad's long effort to make biological arms.

THE PROLOGUE: Iraq Renounces Germ War, but ...

In the 1950s and '60s, the world's major armed forces experimented widely with germ warfare. Eventually they concluded that the nightmarish weapons were too repugnant and too difficult to use.

By 1972, the global threat of biological war seemed to recede as Iraq joined the United States, the Soviet Union and more than 100 other nations in signing the Biological and Toxin Weapons Convention. The accord banned possession of deadly biological agents except for defensive work like research into vaccines, detectors and protective gear.

But it was only a pledge. It had no formal means of enforcement and plenty of room for activities that were ambiguous as to whether they were defensive or offensive.

Indeed, Iraq's clandestine effort to acquire biological weapons, some inspectors now suspect, actually began shortly after it lent its support to the convention.

Unlike nuclear arms, dangerous germs are cheap and easy to come by.

The allure was great. Unlike nuclear arms, dangerous germs are cheap and easy to come by. Yet their effects on people are potentially just as extensive and grim as those of a nuclear bomb, if slower to act. A microbe that divides every 30 minutes can produce more than a billion descendants in hours, and a bubbling vat of offspring in a week or so. Even a few can be dangerous.

Anthrax, normally a disease of cattle and sheep, can kill a human after exposure to less than 10,000 germs, all of which would fit comfortably on the period at the end of this sentence. Signs of pulmonary anthrax infection include high fever, labored breathing and vomiting. It is usually fatal within two weeks. A vaccine can prevent the infection, and it can be treated with huge doses of antibiotics if caught in its early stages.

U.S. military and intelligence officials in the 1980s gathered much evidence that Iraq had developed a large program to build biological arms, with the work focused on anthrax.

The West tried to block the effort. In 1988 the Iraqis ordered a 1,325-gallon fermenter to grow germs from a Swiss company, Chemap, and arranged to buy several more. But the United States and its allies persuaded Switzerland to drop the sale, said Dr. Jonathan B. Tucker, a former federal arms-control official who is now a germ-weapon expert at the Monterey Institute of International Studies in California.

The perceived threat was so great that on the eve of the gulf war, President George Bush warned Saddam that Iraq would pay a "terrible price" if it used biological or chemical weapons.

But the intelligence about germ warfare was generally imprecise, and as the U.S.-led coalition prepared for war after Iraq's invasion of Kuwait in 1990, planners could identify only one potential germ factory in Iraq. That site, Salman Pak, not far from Baghdad, was bombed in the gulf war.

Though only one factory was identified, the U.S. military started a crash program to vaccinate as many troops as possible against anthrax and opened a campaign to knock out refrigerated bunkers suspected of holding biological arms. After the war, U.S. officials were embarrassed to find that the suspicious bunkers held only conventional arms, sheltered from the desert sun.

After losing the war, Saddam, as a condition of surrender, agreed to declare within 15 days all his nuclear, chemical and biological arms and the long-range missiles needed to deliver them, and then to destroy them all.

The United Nations set up a group to make sure he kept his word. Until it verified destruction of the weapons, Iraq was barred from selling oil, virtually its sole source of foreign exchange.

Later, the United Nations relented a bit and allowed some oil exports to pay for food and medicine and to make reparations to Kuwait.

THE HUNT: Hide and Seek in the Wilds

Dozens of science detectives, many with military backgrounds, were assembled from several nations after the war to discover the truth about the biological arms. The inspectors, men and women ranging in age from their 20s to their 60s, worked out of dingy, roach-and-rat-infested hotels in Baghdad.

Their first foray was to Salman Pak, a town and military center southeast of Baghdad on an isolated bend of the Tigris River. About 30 inspectors with the commission, known as Unscom, went there in August 1991 because the site was considered the heart of Iraq's germ-warfare complex.

Sheltered by high walls, air defenses and a military unit, the installation had been bombed during the war, and inspectors were eager for a close-up look at what remained.

They were shocked, inspectors recalled. Two weeks before the team's arrival, the Iraqis had leveled much of the site, removing production gear, demolishing two buildings and bulldozing the rubble. Piles of ashes and melted binders suggested that the Iraqis had kindled bonfires of documents.

Iraqi officials insisted that research at the site was peaceful, intended to develop vaccines and other protection against dread diseases.

But the investigators suspected the site had a military purpose, and eventually found a chamber for dispersing germs on test subjects that was big enough to hold "large primates, including the human primate," one inspector recalled.

The Iraqis said the chamber had been used merely for testing the effectiveness of vaccines on such animals as sheep, donkeys, monkeys and dogs. But they had hauled the chamber to a garbage dump some 20 miles from Salman Pak and then crushed it with a bulldozer, apparently trying to keep it out of sight.

Tucker, of the Monterey Institute, a former Unscom member, said the inspectors had detected "a pattern of circumstantial evidence" of germ-weapon production at Salman Pak but had found no smoking gun.

While at Salman Pak, the Iraqis told the inspectors of another plant at Al Hakam, a site an hour's drive southwest of Baghdad that sprawled across seven square miles of isolated desert.

Filling some of the buildings at Al Hakam were mazes of pipes, valves, pumps and stainless-steel tanks. The Iraqis said they were for making animal feed and bacterial pesticide. But the buildings were spaced unusually far apart and surrounded by barbed wire, dummy bunkers, air defenses and many guard posts.

Again, the evidence was equivocal. The inspectors suspected much but had no proof.

In May 1992, Baghdad finally gave the United Nations its first "full, final and complete disclosure" about its germ program, a report in which Baghdad denied having ever dabbled in any kind of biological arms and called for the inspections and sanctions to end.

Though the germ team kept running into dead ends, their colleagues seeking other types of weapons kept making breakthroughs. Inspectors seeking chemical arms found arsenals full of nerve agents like tabun and sarin, tiny amounts of which are lethal. And to their shock, nuclear teams found Iraq had made considerable progress in building an atomic bomb.

The germ sleuthing from 1991 to 1994 was hindered, in part, by the lack of experienced professionals at headquarters in New York to direct the effort: Three years after the gulf war, the headquarters still had no full-time staff biologist.

But congressional investigators were zooming ahead. By early 1994, they had learned that the American Type Culture Collection, a company in Rockville, Md., that sells microbes to scientists, had shipped up to 36 stains of 10 deadly pathogens to Iraq in the 1980s, doing so with government approval. Some had come from Fort Detrick, Md., the Army's main center for defensive germ research.

"I was horrified," recalled James J. Tuite III, a congressional aide who tracked the shipments for Sen. Donald Riegle, D-Mich., then chairman of the Senate Banking Committee. "These were clearly agents that could be used for biological warfare." Arguably, they also had use in making vaccines, though experts with access to intelligence data about Baghdad's ambitions doubted that explanation.

THE SLEUTH: Trying to Unravel a Tangle of Clues

In April 1994, under increasing pressure from the United Nations to come up with something or drop the germ investigation, Unscom hired Dr. Richard Spertzel, who soon became the head of the biological team.

A portly man of military bearing, Spertzel, then 61, had served for nearly three decades in the Army before retiring in 1987 as a colonel. For 21 years he had worked in the world of military germs, both defensive and offensive, much of the time at Fort Detrick.

Spertzel brought valuable expertise. He belonged to a generation that knew about germ weapons from personal experience, from the days when the United States had made them and envisioned their use in war.

By all accounts, Spertzel re-energized the Iraq inquiry. He pored over documents—"the evidence was almost shouting out," he recalled—and took his worries to Rolf Ekeus, the Swedish diplomat who then headed the United Nations effort to eliminate Iraq's weapons systems.

Ekeus ordered new inspection teams into the Iraqi hinterlands. But he also warned Spertzel that they had to find evidence of military germs soon, or give Iraq a clean bill of health.

By November 1994, Spertzel and three other experts in Iraq were interviewing and re-interviewing Iraqi scientists, picking apart their accounts and analyzing statements and records for discrepancies.

The team included Dr. David Kelly, a former Oxford University microbiologist; Barton, the Australian biologist, and Lt. Col. Hamish Killip, of the British Royal Engineers. They came together in argumentative camaraderie, at times calling themselves the Gang of Four.

The team soon uncovered a secretive Iraqi group known as the Technical and Scientific Materials Import Division. Part of the Organization of Military Industrialization, it appeared to focus on germ warfare; for instance, it supplied Salman Pak. The inspectors immediately knew the discovery was significant.

"We were all very awake," recalled Barton, who recently left the U.N. commission.

With that high card, the team was able to conduct a very narrow, pointed search for records. To aid its hunt, the commission wrote in December 1994 to a handful of nations seeking help in uncovering documents about sales of biological materials to that Iraqi group.

One reply came from Israel, said two U.S. intelligence experts familiar with the episode, confirming a recent account of it in the *Times of London*. The Israelis provided key trade documents that helped illuminate a central if seemingly mundane foundation of the Iraqi germ program—microbial food.

The nutrients that bacteriologists use to feed and breed germs are known as growth media. A specialized blend of sugars, proteins and minerals that keep microscopic life flourishing, growth media have many legitimate uses in hospitals and clinics, mainly as a way to identify illnesses. For instance, a swab from the back of a patient's throat is placed in a small dish of diagnostic media, and the presence of disease germs is indicated by the visible growth of bacterial colonies.

But Iraq was found to have been importing growth media by the ton, enough for growing teeming hordes of germs and filling many hundreds of biological weapons, if not thousands.

The intelligence experts and the *London Times* report said the Israelis had documented exports in the 1980s to Iraq from Oxoid, a British company. Israel, the experts said, provided two letters of credit that referred to sales of about 10 tons of growth media to Iraq.

The documents were vital in building a case that Iraq had produced biological weapons. The inspectors, who under U.N. rules cannot talk about companies or countries other than Iraq, refused to discuss how the documents were obtained but emphasized their importance.

"That clinched it," said Kelly, the former Oxford don.

Spertzel, the chief biological inspector, called it "breakthrough information, frankly," adding, "It was conclusive enough to sit down with Iraq and be very challenging."

Barton used the bank documents to play his bluff in January 1995—and it worked. Almost immediately, Baghdad acknowledged the purchases and produced evidence that it had bought even more germ nutrients. All told, from Iraq and other sources, the team eventually found that Iraq had imported about 40 tons of growth media, roughly 30 times more than needed for any conceivable civilian uses.

And where was it now?

Iraqi officials had an answer. It was for regional hospitals and laboratories that were making vaccines and detecting diseases.

Spertzel asked Gabriele Kraatz-Wadsack, 44, a German member of the team, to test that explanation. During March 1995, she and her team tracked down the growth media at warehouses and pharmaceutical factories; much of it turned out to be stored at Al Hakam, the big plant in the desert.

"But I could still only account for 22 to 23 tons," she recalled. "That meant that more than 17 tons were missing."

Clearly, Baghdad had more explaining to do. Tensions rose. Eventually the Iraqis said much of the growth media sent to hospitals had been destroyed in riots after the 1991 war.

As the team kept up the pressure, the Iraqis panicked. The meetings between Unscom members and the Iraqi officials turned into shouting matches. "It was a free-for-all," Barton said.

The breakthrough came on July 1, 1995, at an evening session in Baghdad. Dr. Rihab Taha, an acknowledged leader of Iraq's civilian germ effort, made a huge admission. It came grudgingly, inspectors said, and with no direct eye contact. Taha kept looking down at her notes as she spoke.

Yes, she said, almost in tears at the strain of the moment, Iraq had produced a horde of germs for biological warfare.

Iraq had imported about 40 tons of growth media, roughly 30 times more than needed for any conceivable civilian uses.

An eerie quiet followed. Inspectors wanted to ask questions but refrained.

"There was not a lot of discussion," Barton recalled. "None of us thought we would hear a real confession."

The Iraqis acknowledged, among other things, that the factory at Al Hakam had produced thousands of gallons of deadly anthrax and botulinum toxin—enough, in theory, to wipe out whole cities and even nations.

For the first time, the Iraqis had confessed to a military program for making germs. But no more than that. They still denied having ever developed weapons designed to release those germs over enemy targets.

THE DEFECTOR: A Breakthrough in a Chicken Coop

The overlord of the Organization of Military Industrialization was Lt. Gen. Hussein Kamal, Saddam's son-in-law and the second most powerful man in Iraq. He had risen from a lowly bodyguard to become director of Iraq's advanced-weapons procurement program and reportedly had a personality almost as swaggering and domineering as his father-in-law's, seeing himself as the natural successor.

Al Hakam had been his pet project, the inspectors learned, a personal triumph with which he planned to increase his prestige in the feuding family that ruled Iraq. But now, in early July 1995, his subordinates had been forced to reveal its dark purpose.

After Taha's dramatic admission, Iraq gave the U.N. team an ultimatum. According to team members, the Iraqis demanded that the United Nations bring all inspections to an end within a month. If not, the inspectors would have to go. The Iraqi ambassador who delivered the message said he was speaking on behalf of Kamal.

The inspectors replied that quick settlement was impossible given the new questions swirling around the germ work.

Iraqi threats mounted, and the inspectors prepared to leave Baghdad, some fearing for their safety.

"He was in an impossible situation," Barton said of Kamal. "He had given us an absurd ultimatum."

Then, suddenly, everything changed.

Late on the evening of Aug. 7, 1995, Kamal defected to Jordan. The move reportedly occurred after he had quarreled at a family dinner that was called to discuss Iraq's worsening economy and security, and that ended with shooting that left six bodyguards dead. After that he fled.

For the first time, the Iraqis had confessed to a military program for making germs.

Inspectors said his flight was caused partly by their discovery of his biological weapons program, which damaged his standing with the ruling family.

Seeking to pre-empt any disclosures, Baghdad withdrew its ultimatum and, on Aug. 20, presented a trove of documents that it said "the traitor General Kamal," as they now called him, had hidden from the Iraqi government.

To reinforce the accusations against the general, the handing over of the documents took place at a shed on Kamal's chicken farm.

The documents ran to more that half a million pages, stored in boxes and steel trunks. There was a single, small, wooden box of documents about the biological-weapons program. Though far from complete, the papers showed that Iraq had done nearly everything in its power to prepare and use biological weapons.

In documents and additional admissions that year, Iraq said it had taken these actions:

* Set its germ policy in 1974, seeking to build a stockpile of biological arms.
* Did research on anthrax, botulinium toxin (which causes muscular paralysis resulting in death), aflatoxin (which causes liver cancer), tricothecene mycotoxins (which cause nausea, vomiting and diarrhea), wheat cover smut (which ruins food grains), hemorrhagic conjunctivitis (which causes extreme pain and temporary blindness) and rotavirus (which causes acute diarrhea that can lead to death).
* Field-tested germs in sprayers, 122-mm rockets, 155-millimeter artillery shells, tanks dropped from jet fighters and LD-250 aerial bombs.
* Began a crash program to speed germ development in August 1990, just as it invaded Kuwait.
* Built and loaded 25 germ warheads for Al Hussein missiles, which have a range of 400 miles. Botulinum toxin went into 16 of them, anthrax into 5 and aflatoxin into 4. The warheads were about 3 feet wide and 10 feet long. It also filled bombs designated R-400, which hold 20 gallons each. Botulinum toxin went into 100, anthrax into 50 and aflatoxin into 7.
* Deployed these weapons in the opening days of the 1991 gulf war at four locations, ready for use, and kept them there throughout the war.

Iraq also said it had secretly destroyed all its biological agents and weapons in May or June 1991. This was a violation of the surrender agreement, and inspectors express serious doubts about the truth of that admission.

The date of the purported destruction was vague, Iraqi officials said, because no one could remember exactly when the order was given and no records were kept of the event.

After the defection of Kamal and the chicken-farm revelations, the U.N. inspectors and the Iraqis involved in germ warfare forged closer cooperation. Some inspectors feared that the honeymoon might not last, "so we decided to collect as much information as possible," Barton said. "We were vacuum cleaners."

In May 1996 the Iraqis, under U.N. supervision, began destroying Al Hakam, cutting up machinery with torches, burying items in cement and then dynamiting the rest of the plant. And the next month Iraq filed its fourth "full, final and complete disclosure," only to have the inspectors again dismiss it as sloppy lies.

U.N. officials eventually identified seven sites that had been directly used to produce biological weapons, including Salman Pak and Al Hakam.

In addition, the inspectors began monitoring universities, diagnostic laboratories and research centers, and installations that made vaccines, pharmaceuticals, beer and dairy products. All told, the United Nations was keeping its eye on about 100 Iraq sites, most with civilian equipment that could be turned to making germ weapons.

As for Kamal, he eventually returned to Iraq, repentant over his defection. Days later, he and his family died from gunshot wounds. Reports from Iraq said family members had turned on him. But the circumstances of his death remain unclear.

THE MYSTERIES: Germ-War Capacity Is Still an Enigma

Overlooking the East River in New York, on the 30th and 31st floors of the U.N. building, is the inspectors' headquarters. The windowless conference room, known as the Bunker, is constantly jammed these days. Cubicles are packed with file cabinets and safes and documents. Wooden crates from the chicken farm are visible atop cabinets, part of a mountain of evidence.

Over the years the United Nations commission, whose staff is drawn from more than 30 different countries, has become a lightening rod for Iraqi criticism. Its inspectors are routinely vilified by name in the government-controlled press as spies. Some nations sympathetic to Iraq's plight, including

Russia, have complained that the inspectors are overly aggressive and are taking too long. The inspectors, in response, have at times fired back, discussing their work with the news media.

U.N. officials say the inspectors still differ over how to interpret the evidence. Perhaps the most contentious issue is whether Iraq is now engaged in germ procurement and production.

The Russians recently acknowledged holding talks with Iraq in 1995 about selling a huge plant to be installed at Al Hakam, and inspectors say they have evidence of other buying discussions and sales.

Sprayers are an important part of the current mystery. Planes flying over farms use pipes and nozzles to spray fine mists of liquid pesticides on crops. The Iraqis, an inspector said, have admitted adapting at least six sprayers to make a mist of germs that would rain down on enemies, and importing parts for a dozen such conversions in all.

But the agricultural sprayers, he said, have disappeared. None have been turned over to inspectors, and their whereabouts and status are unknown—whether lost or destroyed or ready to fly into action.

A pilotless plane spraying 200 pounds of anthrax near a large city might kill up to a million people.

Are they a threat? Even if they exist, hidden by the Iraqi military, their effective use is clouded by huge uncertainties, inspectors said. A pilotless plane spraying 200 pounds of anthrax near a large city might kill up to a million people—if the winds were right, if no rain fell, if the nozzles did not get clogged, if the particles were the right size, if the population had no vaccinations, and so on.

Iraq tried to develop just such a weapon, using a sprayer of Iraqi design. Barton said an Iraqi general had told inspectors that Baghdad had tried just before the gulf war to develop the capability to wipe out out most of Israel's population. MiG fighters were modified so they could be flown over Israel by remote control to release a spray of anthrax from specially modified fuel tanks.

"It would have caused massive casualties," he said, "if it was workable."

That kind of hedge appears in many of the analyses about Iraqi systems for dispensing germs, and it is a crucial unknown in assessing how far Iraq progressed toward making effective biological arms. The problem for the inspectors is that they have only limited information about how the dispensing systems would perform in war.

The inspectors agree that unless they can go anywhere in Iraq without notice to hunt for documents, scientists and equipment, the United Nations can offer the world only a false sense of security.

There are doubts about whether the latest agreement, negotiated over the weekend by U.N. Secretary General Kofi Annan, provides sufficient access. Under the accord, the inspectors can visit the "presidential sites" that Iraq declared off-limits last fall. But they will be accompanied by diplomats appointed by the Security Council, and they must honor Iraq's "national security, sovereignty and dignity."

But while inspectors may disagree about what Iraq is doing now, there is no disagreement about Baghdad's potential to develop biological weapons.

Worry about Iraq's potential has been reinforced by what most inspectors agree is Baghdad's refusal in recent years to provide further documents about its biological program.

"Most of us agree that if Unscom monitors left, the Iraqis could start up a biological weapons program the next day," Barton said.

Worry about Iraq's potential has been reinforced by what most inspectors agree is Baghdad's refusal in recent years to provide further documents about its biological program. Few inspectors seem to believe Iraq's assertions that most of the documents have been destroyed.

"Every little pencil they purchased has three requisition copies," Graatz-Wadsack said. "We've found documents in other programs going back to the late 1950s. So I don't believe they destroyed their biological documents. They have them hidden somewhere."

Inspectors see the missing documents as key to understanding the true dimensions of Iraq's effort to make germ weapons, saying they might provide a map to hidden plants, personnel and arms. The documents, inspectors say, are also useful to Iraq because they are thought to form a blueprint for resuming production of germ weapons.

Inspection teams may have been getting close to those records when Iraq began refusing the United Nations access to some sites last October. The inspectors also agree that as long as Iraq denies the inspectors access and information, they may never be able to certify that Baghdad is harboring no more germ weapons.

"I once asked: 'Is there an end game?'" Barton recalled. "We've been lied to so many times, can we ever trust the Iraqis to tell us the truth?"

Secret Casualties of the Gulf[5]

There's a good reason why our government tends to deny claims that our troops were exposed to chemical attack in the war—because they were, a former CIA analyst claims.

Satellites wheeled silently in the cold vacuum of space, snapping photographs above the Persian Gulf and sending them back to intelligence analysts in the United States. These photographs showed clearly enemy troop movements and the deployment of kinghell weaponry to the frontlines, including Scud missile placements, in anticipation of the invasion that was certain to come.

The chilling variable that had many sweating and wringing their hands at the Pentagon and Central Intelligence Agency was the image no satellite camera could capture—the unpredictability of Saddam Hussein and his high command: Would they order chemical agents be packed into the warheads of the Scuds and artillery and fired at U.S.-led coalition forces? It was a plausible concern since Hussein was accused of using such weapons in the long war against the Iranians—he even had unleashed killer gas on his own people in northern Iraq as a way to squash a rebellion.

Patrick and Robin Eddington, a husband and wife who analyzed satellite imagery for the CIA during the war, are convinced our troops were not only exposed to the residual effects of chemicals from the destruction of Iraqi ammo bunkers, but also sustained direct chemical attacks. The Eddingtons also allege the Department of Defense (DoD) and their former employer have pursued a policy of "deceit and disinformation" in debunking claims that thousands of ailing Desert Storm veterans are casualties of secret chemical warfare.

"The evidence of chemical exposure is overwhelming," says Patrick Eddington.

"The evidence of chemical exposure is overwhelming," says Patrick Eddington, relaxing in a living-room of his Fairfax, VA home. "Yet, our government continues to deny it and deal with it. How is it our government will take the word of a Kurd (in northern Iraq) who says he was a gas attack victim and yet turn its back on our own people who were in the field and reported the same thing? It's unconscionable to me

---

5. Article by Joe Stuteville for the *American Legion* magazine p34-35 Mar. 1997. Copyright © 1997 American Legion Magazine. Reprinted with permission.

and a slap in the face to every American who has ever put his or her life an the line in combat."

During the war, field commanders filed reports of chemical detections, but strategists running the show in Riyadh, Saudi Arabia, and at home in the United States downplayed—denied—that such exposures occurred. In recent months, DoD has acknowledged that more than 20,000 troops might have been exposed to residual nerve agents following the post-war destruction of an enemy bunker complex near Khamisiyah in southern Iraq.

One thing is certain about those who served in the gulf: Many today continue to suffer from unexplained chronic fatigue and flu-like symptoms, digestive and respiratory problems, hair loss and aching joints. Research into what could be causing many of their ills is ongoing with more than 70 independent studies investigating all potential causes, including chemical agent exposures, anti-nerve agent inoculations U.S. troops were given when they were deployed to the gulf region, exposure to fallout from burning oil wells and other toxic wastes. Some researchers have suggested many of the troops' health problems might be linked to a combination of the above and other environmental factors.

Eddington, 33, went to work with the CIA in 1988, after service as an armor officer in the Army Reserves. While in training at the CIA's photoanalysis school, he met his future wife, Robin Katzman, who recently had graduated from Brandeis University. After their training, both went to work and excelled at their positions with the agency.

For Patrick Eddington, the training was put to the test when Iraqi troops rumbled into Kuwait in August 1990 and launched a reign of terror in the oil-rich emirate. Before the war ignited and as both sides continued their buildup, Eddington says intelligence clearly showed Iraq had moved chemical weapons to the front—and intended to use them.

"The intelligence I reviewed after the war showed that there may have been between eight to 12 chemical attacks on our troops, most likely released from exploding Scud missiles and from aircraft penetrations and artillery attacks," says Patrick Eddington. In 1994, the Eddingtons embarked on their own investigation of exposures based on about 300 classified documents, of which about 60 eventually found theit way to the public via the DoD website, GulfLINK.

Before the war ignited and as both sides continued their buildup, Eddington says intelligence clearly showed Iraq had moved chemical weapons to the front—and intended to use them.

Patrick Eddington is not alone in his assessment of Iraq's chemical arsenal. In an interview with the *American Legion* magazine last year, Dr. Jonathan B. Tucker, a former chemical and biological weapons expert for the congressional Office of Technology Assessment said declassified logs of the 1st and 2nd Marine Divisions and the Army's 101st Airborne Division indicated numerous detections of gas and mustard agents, and that chemical munitions were frequently discovered in abandoned Iraqi bunkers and vehicles.

Tucker, who was a member of the United Nations chemical and weapons inspection team in Iraq after the war, says Iraq possessed a veritable killer gumbo of chemical weapons: hundreds of tons of mustard agents and four types of nerve agents—sarin, tabun, GF and VX, not to mention tens of thousands of liters of biological agents which were loaded into Iraqi bombs and the warheads of Al-Hussein missiles, an extended-range Scud. If such weapons were used, even just a few, why then weren't there massive and widespread deaths and casualties among coalition forces?

"Iraqi military planners recognized that it is more disruptive to the enemy to injure and debilitate rather than to kill, because dead soldiers require less attention and resources than wounded ones," Tucker says.

Patrick Eddington says there are two grim and compelling reasons why the government would stonewall on the chemical exposure issue. First, in his own research, he says he found U.S. military documents revealing that some of the Iraqi chemical weapons found bore the markings of having been produced by U.S. firms—agents and components that might have been sold to Iraq during its war with Iran.

Second, is a matter of military resolve on the battlefield. When Hussein threatened to let loose with a barrage of chemical weapons on the eve of the war, the United States and its allies said the response would render Iraq a battered wasteland.

"In other words, if you accept that Iraq got away with gassing our people, what kind of message does this send to rogue nations such as Iran, North Korea and Syria?" Eddington says, "We're an open target in future conflicts because we are perceived as weak and unwilling to live up to [threats of] retaliation."

Armed with documents and other intelligence gathered during his own probe of chemical usage in the gulf, Patrick Eddington took the logical step. He presented the information to his CIA superiors in July 1994, recommending the agency review its earlier findings.

"My immediate supervisor was quite upset that I had been Only my assurance that it had not interfered with my reguly duties 'prevented me' from getting into hot water."

In the meantime, the Eddingtons continued to sift through the information and search for more evidence to support their claims. They waited for a response from the agency and learned from another analyst about the status of the report. "This person informed us the agency was determined to debunk the information."

Angered and disappointed after learning about the CIA's alleged stonewalling on the issue, Patrick Eddington went public with his concerns. On Dec. 7, 1994, a letter that perhaps will live in infamy, was published in the *Washington Times*. Writing as a citizen and not as a CIA insider, Eddington said the government was instigating a "cover-up" about the extent to which U.S. forces were exposed to chemical agents in the Persian Gulf. He suggested the DoD was "negligent and obstructionist" on the issue of health problems suffered by gulf veterans.

The Eddingtons' work apparently was gnawing at the nerves among some CIA brass.

A few months later, the Eddingtons were asked to brief CIA officials about their findings. Shortly after that, Patrick Eddington was asked to give a similar briefing to a former top general of the Army's 7th Corps deployed to the gulf. "I ran into a buzzsaw before I started my briefing," Eddington recalls. "He told me I didn't have a case and was stirring up trouble for no good reason. End of case."

In October 1995, Eddington was allowed to give a classified briefing at CIA headquarters in Langley, Va., before Jonathan Tucker and Holly Gwin, members of the Presidential Advisory Committee on Gulf War Veterans' Illnesses. Some of that information was expected to be included in its final report, which, at press time, had not been made public. When contacted by the *American Legion Magazine*, the committee declined to comment on the preliminary findings or details of its report.

The Eddingtons' work apparently was gnawing at the nerves among some CIA brass. Patrick Eddington says he learned in early 1996 that he was the target of a criminal investigation by the CIA, seeking to determine if he had leaked classified information with the publication of his letter in the *Washington Times*. Eddington says the agency found no wrongdoing on his part.

With great reluctance and the perceived reality that their careers were all but over, the Eddingtons turned in their resignations to their CIA bosses last October. "It was something I didn't want to do, but the handwriting was on the wall," says Patrick Eddington. "It was a difficult desicion personally—for both of us.

The Eddingtons have since finished writing a book about his probe, *Gassed in the Gulf* (Insignia Publishing, Suite 535, 1429 G St., NW, Washington, DC, 20005, (800) 606-BOOK #2665). Robin Eddington has since gone to work for a private defense contractor; Patrick remains unemployed.

Meanwhile, the CIA and DoD have been trying to defuse the explosive accounts that they have concealed information about chemical exposures and other claims made by the Eddingtons. In a rare news conference in late 1996, the CIA responded: "Their findings just did not pass peer review," said CIA spokesman David Christian, referring to an internal review of the Eddingtons' report. "To label a difference of opinion [as a coverup] is just unfair, illogical and plain wrong."

DoD also has gone on the defensive. "The Pentagon has nothing to hide, and I think that's clear from our performance in the past several months," said DoD spokesman Kenneth Bacon in an Oct. 31 1996, news conference. "We have been aggressive in releasing information. We have no evidence that Iraq used chemical or biological weapons in the Gulf War. . . The Iraqis themselves said they did not use chemical weapons in the war."

Indeed, Iraq seems a strange source to cite as credible. Wasn't it Saddam Hussein, who denies using chemicals in the war with Iran, who gave the orders to unleash a killer chemical attack against Kurdish toddlers and mothers as a means to deal with unruly rebels in his own country?

And isn't this the same crowd that stonewalled for time and harangued U.N. inspectors assigned to weapons sites in Iraq?

As for Patrick and Robin Eddington, their preferred sources are the thousands of Americans who put their lives on the line in the Persian Gulf six years ago. "I'm a veteran and it hurts me to think that—my God—these are my fellow veterans who are suffering from a variety of illnesses related to their service. It's criminal if our government is following a deliberate path of turning its back on them."

III. The Chemical Weapons Convention

Editor's Introduction

International agreements to restrict chemical weapons predate the 20th century. The Hague Convention of 1907 is among the first attempts made in the modern era. However, the carnage caused by poison gas in World War I proved the Hague Convention ineffective. Seven years after the conclusion of the war, the nations of the world approved the Geneva Protocol, which was perhaps the most important and far-reaching agreement of its kind. Nevertheless, there were loopholes: while it prohibited the use of biological and chemical weapons, it permitted the stockpiling of such weapons, and provided no punishment for nations that violated its provisions.

In 1990, the nations of the world, led by the United States and the Soviet Union, began work on the Chemical Weapons Convention (CWC), an agreement which would have much more stringent restrictions than anything before. Not only would the use of chemical weapons be banned, but their development and stockpiling would be as well. The convention would call for the destruction of all existing weapons, and allow for the penalization of violating nations. In 1997, after years of negotiations, the treaty was ratified by 65 nations including the U.S. However, debate continues as to the merits and drawbacks of this new protocol. In the articles presented in this chapter, I have tried to represent both sides of this heated issue.

The first piece is a special report given before the Senate Foreign Relations Committee by Baker Spring, a policy analyst for the Heritage Foundation, entitled "The Chemical Weapons Convention: A Bad Deal for America." The report was given in April 1996, one year before the ratification of the treaty. Spring provides background information on what led up to the formulation of the CWC, as well as a summary of its provisions. Then, through a series of self-answered questions, he explains why he believes the CWC would actually make matters worse for the United States as far as the threat of chemical warfare is concerned. In addition to his reasons for opposing the treaty, he also proposes his own alternative methods for preventing the proliferation of chemical weapons.

The second anti-CWC piece is an article by Douglas J. Feith entitled "Chemical Reaction." Writing for the *New Republic*, one month before the treaty's ratification, Feith disputes what he describes as the Senate's "better-than-nothing" attitude toward the CWC. He argues that the convention would actually increase the development of chemical weapons by eliminating export controls, which he believes have been much more effective than the proposed ban. Feith also postulates that international trafficking in chemical weapons would also be made easier under the CWC.

Providing an argument in favor of the CWC is "Stay the Course on the Chemical Weapons Ban," an article by Amy E. Smithson from *Issues in Science and Technology*.

The piece was written several months after the ratification of the CWC, and addresses what the author describes as the federal government's attempts to "water down" the treaty's provisions. Smithson criticizes Congress for failing to pass legislation for implementing CWC regulations on time, thus denying chemical companies the necessary guidelines to fulfill their requirements. She also reports on some of the positive results of the treaty, thus stressing the advantages to be gained through full cooperation.

"Ratify the Chemical Weapons Convention" is an editorial by Floyd E. Bloom of *Science* magazine, and the second pro-CWC piece in this chapter. Bloom, echoing the opinions of the overwhelming majority of the scientific community, calls for the United States to back the convention. The author stresses the diplomatic, economic and scientific benefits of supporting the CWC, and urges that our nation not remain among the group of nations who had yet to ratify the treaty, including North Korea, Libya, and Iran.

Rounding out the chapter is "Cleansing Job," which appeared in the *Economist*. Neither for nor against the treaty, the article recounts a specific instance of a nation attempting to comply with CWC regulations. In this case, it is the daunting task that faced Japan in 1997: disposing of the thousands of gas-filled shells left behind in China at the end of World War II. At the time the piece was written, China had not signed the treaty, but was negotiating with Japan as to how to eliminate the weapons. Japan's efforts at the time of the article are described, including plans to build a processing plant in China's Jilin province.

The Chemical Weapons Convention: A Bad Deal for America[1]

THE DECADES-LONG EFFORT TO BAN CHEMICAL WEAPONS

The history behind the Chemical Weapons Convention is a long and tortuous one. It has long been the aim of diplomats to curtail both the use and stockpiling of chemical weapons. Among the earliest attempts in modern times to ban the use of chemical weapons was the 1907 Hague Convention. Approved by the European powers, the convention prohibited the use of weapons containing poison, but the widespread use of chemical weapons in World War I proved that this prohibition had little effect. After the war, a League of Nations conference convened in Switzerland to approve the 1925 Geneva Protocol, which prohibited the use of both biological and chemical weapons in war, but not their development, production, and stockpiling. Among the countries signing the Geneva Protocol were the United States, France, Germany, Britain, Italy, and Japan. Unlike the 1907 Hague Convention, the Geneva Protocol was successful once war broke out. Chemical weapons were not used widely during World War II, but this success was due to implicit threats by allied leaders, particularly President Franklin Roosevelt, to respond in kind to any chemical attack. It is one of history's clearest examples of a successful deterrence policy.

The Geneva Protocol is still in force, and the U.S. honors its terms, although it did not ratify the protocol until 1975.

The Geneva Protocol is still in force, and the U.S. honors its terms, although it did not ratify the protocol until 1975. It is, however, a weak agreement. If countries violate it, they remain unpunished, and there are no established procedures for determining the veracity of reported claims of biological or chemical weapons use. It is sometimes referred to as the "no first use" agreement because participating states agreed to comply with its terms so long as biological or chemical weapons were not used against them first. Some states, including the U.S., ratified the agreement with the reserva-

---

1. By Baker Spring, senior policy analyst, for the Heritage Foundation Web site Apr. 15, 1996. Copyright © 1996 the Heritage Foundation. It can be viewed online at http://www.heritage.org/library/categories/natsec/cb25.html.

tion that it would cease to be binding if they were attacked first.

Violations of the Geneva Protocol have occurred on several occasions since the end of World War II. The Soviet Union and its clients, for example, used mycotoxins, commonly referred to as "yellow rain," against civilians in Afghanistan and Southeast Asia in the 1970s and 1980s, and Iraq used chemical weapons during its eight-year war with Iran in the 1980s.

Negotiations leading to the Chemical Weapons Convention began in 1971 when the U.N. Conference on Disarmament's predecessor organization, the Eighteen-Nation Disarmament Committee, voted to conduct separate talks on banning biological and chemical weapons. This allowed for the conclusion in 1992 of the Biological Weapons Convention, which banned the production and stockpiling of biological and toxin weapons, but put negotiations to ban chemical weapons on the back burner for well over a decade.

Diplomatic efforts in the 1980s focused on stopping the spread of chemical weapons to Third World countries.

By the mid-1980s, the Reagan Administration, expressing concern over the large-scale Soviet chemical weapons program, began producing a new generation of chemical munitions for the U.S. military. The subsequent U.S. program was legal because the 1925 Geneva Protocol outlawed only the use, not the development, production, and stockpiling, of chemical munitions.

Diplomatic efforts in the 1980s focused on stopping the spread of chemical weapons to Third World countries. In 1984, Australia proposed to establish controls on the export of ingredients that could be used to manufacture chemical weapons. This proposal was made to the Organization for Economic Cooperation and Development (OECD), an organization of the industrialized states to coordinate economic development policies for the Third World. The Australians wanted participating countries to coordinate export control policies to stem the transfer of chemical weapons-related technologies to the Third World. Specific restrictions and enforcement mechanisms were left to individual governments. The "Australia Group" now has 29 members, including such prominent nations as the U.S., France, Britain, and Japan.

The informal and voluntary nature of the Australian proposal has limited its effectiveness. For example, the enforcement of the export restrictions falls to individual member governments, but industrialized nations have a spotty record on how vigorously they enforce export restrictions. In the 1980s, a Phillips Petroleum Company subsidiary in Belgium delivered the chemical thiodiglycol (used in manufacturing mustard gas) to Iraq, and Britain is reported to have sold thiodiglycol and thionyl chloride to Iraq in 1988 and 1989. Both transfers were contrary to the commitments made by Belgium and Britain in the Australia Group. Export control policies, while useful to pursue, by themselves cannot stop the spread of chemical weapons.

President George Bush came to office determined to ban chemical weapons. President Bush and Soviet President Mikhail Gorbachev signed an agreement on June 1, 1990, in Washington to reduce the chemical stockpiles of the U.S. and the Soviet Union to 5,000 metric tons each. No accord, however, was reached outlining inspection procedures for confirming the destruction of these weapons. That was left to subsequent negotiations, which were supposed to be completed by December 31, 1990. This deadline passed without agreement between Moscow and Washington, and the "bilateral destruction agreement" has yet to be brought into force. This failure, to some extent, was due to the turmoil in the Soviet Union, which was collapsing politically. Further, both sides were aware that progress was being made on the Chemical Weapons Convention at the U.N. Conference on Disarmament, and that this convention would have extensive inspection procedures and would ban the weapons entirely.

Despite the setbacks at the bilateral level with Russia, President Bush announced on May 13, 1991, that the U.S. would agree to a complete ban of chemical weapons even if some other nations did not eliminate their arsenals. Bush also pledged that the U.S. would forswear the use of chemical weapons under any circumstances, including situations in which U.S. forces are attacked with such weapons first.

Until that time, Washington had reserved the right to use chemical weapons if attacked with them first and to maintain a chemical weapons stockpile for the purpose of deterrence and possible retaliation. This unilateral concession by the U.S., along with another to drop the demand for stringent "any time, anywhere" inspections of possible chemical weapons facilities, put the Chemical Weapons Convention negotiations on the fast track. The final draft of the convention was completed on September 3, 1991, in Geneva. It was signed in Paris by more than the 65 countries required for ratification to bring the convention into force, including by the United States. Now the Senate, in fulfilling its role to advise and consent to all treaties, must decide whether the United States will ratify the Chemical Weapons Convention.

PROVISIONS OF THE CHEMICAL WEAPONS CONVENTION

I think it would be useful to review the content of the Chemical Weapons Convention. The purpose of the convention is to ban chemical weapons and forbid their production, stockpiling, and use by participating states. It would do so by establishing elaborate procedures for eliminating all chemical weapons no later than ten years after the convention enters into force and by requiring the elimination of chemical weapons production facilities within the same ten-year period. The convention, however, does not require the destruction of toxic chemicals, their precursors (chemicals that can be combined to form toxic chemicals), or facilities that are used for peaceful purposes. Likewise, small stockpiles of lethal chemicals may be retained for the development of defenses against chemical weapons. These chemicals, precursors, and production facilities are subject to verification measures to detect any attempt to convert them into weapons. The convention is of unlimited duration, which is designed to make the destruction of chemical weapons permanent.

The convention is of unlimited duration, which is designed to make the destruction of chemical weapons permanent.

Overseeing the implementation of the agreement will be a large international bureaucracy that in many ways resembles the International Atomic Energy Agency (IAEA), a U.N. agency that fosters cooperation among nations in the peaceful uses of nuclear power. In a similar vein, a new chemical weapons bureaucracy will be created, the Organization for the Prohibition of Chemical Weapons. Headquartered at The Hague, this organization will have three parts. The first will be the Conference of State Parties, consisting of the representatives of all states participating in the convention. It will establish general policies for implementing the convention and will oversee the functions of the organization. The second will be the Executive Council, the executive arm of the organization, consisting of the representatives of 41 participating states picked to achieve geographic balance. The third will be the Technical Secretariat, led by a Director General, which will be responsible for carrying out the inspections to verify compliance.

The first meeting of a commission preparing the groundwork for the chemical weapons organization took place on February 8, 1993, at The Hague. Since that meeting, the Preparatory Commission has focused on building the Provisional Technical Secretariat, the forerunner of the monitoring agency that will be created after the convention comes into force. Activities of the Preparatory Commission thus far have included finding a building to house the agency, establishing inspection procedures, drafting inspection manuals, procuring and testing inspection equipment, and hiring and training inspectors. According to the Arms Control and Disarmament Agency, the 1995 budget for the Preparatory Commission was roughly $17 million, of which the U.S. paid 25 percent. Once up and running, the Organization for the Prohibition of Chemical Weapons will operate at a cost of about $200 million annually. On the basis of a 25 percent contribution, U.S. taxpayers could be expected to pay $50 million annually to support this international organization.

The verification responsibilities of the Technical Secretariat are vast. The convention's Annex on Implementation and Verification (Verification Annex), over 100 pages long, establishes a long list of inspections to verify that chemical weapons and chemical weapons production facilities are destroyed. The Technical Secretariat also is tasked with ensuring that commercial chemical production facilities are not used to develop and produce weapons. The Verification Annex outlines a number of inspection procedures, including the timing of inspections, the appointment of inspectors, the privileges and immunities that governments must extend to inspectors, and the equipment inspectors may bring with them.

The Verification Annex establishes eight different kinds of inspection regimes, all of which must be carried out by the Technical Secretariat. The first kind of inspection verifies whether chemical weapons are destroyed. The second is to verify the destruction or conversion of chemical weapons production facilities. The third, fourth, and fifth kinds of inspections are to detect whether certain types of chemicals have been used in building chemical weapons, based on how easily each of three categories (schedules) of chemicals can be turned into weapons.

The sixth kind of inspection pertains to production facilities that produce chemicals not found in any of the first three schedules. The seventh is the most sensitive insofar as it involves short-notice inspections of states suspected of violating the terms of the convention. The final kind of inspection requires investigating sites where chemical weapons may have been used.

At first, the U.S. demanded that so-called challenge inspections be allowed anywhere and at any time a violation was suspected. It ultimately abandoned this approach in favor of a British proposal for so-called managed access to suspect sites. Under this provision, the inspected state may take steps to guard its national security, as long as they do not involve evading the convention's terms. In order to protect its security, an inspected state may remove sensitive papers; shroud displays and equipment; log off computers; restrict the types of analyses that may be carried out on air, soil, and effluent samples; and even limit which inspectors may gain access to particular areas at a suspect site.

The inspection process is long and involved. It starts with OPCW officials inspecting the locations declared by a member state as weapons sites. The declaration must be filed with the Technical Secretariat no later than 30 days after the convention enters into force. Work on destroying the chemical weapons at the sites must begin within two years and must be completed within ten years.

Once on a weapons site, inspectors will place seals and monitoring devices to guard against a violation. Similar procedures, such as for placing cameras, exist for monitoring whether chemical weapons, production facilities, and non-weapons chemical production facilities have been destroyed. As many as 1,000 inspections a year may be required.

Operating this complex arrangement of inspection regimes will prove costly to U.S. industry and the government. According to expert David Evans of Analytic Services, Inc., of Arlington, Virginia, U.S. industry can be expected to incur costs of between $20 million and $200 million annually to support the inspection process. The higher costs are more likely in the early stages of implementation of the Chemical Weapons Convention. But this general cost to industry assumes that everything goes as planned. If the mechanism in the convention to protect proprietary and other sensitive business information fails, Mr. Evans estimates that the cost to business could exceed $1 billion annually. The U.S. government will have its responsibilities for implementing the convention as the national authority serving as an intermediary between industry and the Organization for Prohibition of Chemical Weapons. The cost of these activities to the U.S. government is estimated to be $25 million annually.

The Chemical Weapons Convention also contains a provision on compliance. The Executive Council bears the responsibility for demanding that a participating state redress a violation. If corrective action is not taken, the Conference of State Parties may suspend the offending state's privileges under the convention. This could include terminating cooperative programs to assist states in developing chemicals for peaceful purposes or denying the offender the right to vote in the Conference of State Parties. In more serious cases of violation, stricter countermeasures would be taken. For example, trade in all chemicals with the offending state could be shut off. In cases where violations pose a threat to the security of other states, the Conference of State Parties may refer the matter to the United Nations General Assembly and the United Nations Security Council. Ultimately, the Security Council serves as the court of final appeal in the enforcement process.

A FIVE-PART TEST OF ARMS CONTROL AGREEMENTS AND THE CHEMICAL WEAPONS CONVENTION

To deserve the support of the Senate, any arms control agreement should pass a five-part test. This test should serve to determine whether a particular arms control agreement meets the minimum standards necessary to serve the national interest. The test consists of five questions, all of which must be answered affirmatively when applied to a particular agreement to insure that it does not contain a fatal flaw. These five questions are: 1) Does the agreement reduce the risk of war? 2) Are the agreement's requirements consistent with U.S. global security responsibilities? 3) Is the agreement adequately verifiable? 4) Is the agreement enforceable? and 5) Does the agreement enhance national security? The Chemical Weapons Convention fails to pass this test in all five particulars.

QUESTION #1: Will the Chemical Weapons Convention reduce the risk of war?

ANSWER #1: By undermining the U.S. chemical deterrent, the Chemical Weapons Convention may increase the likelihood of war or result in the escalation of an existing conflict.

Reducing the level of armaments is not the most important goal of arms control. Reducing the risk of war is far more

By undermining the U.S. chemical deterrent, the Chemical Weapons Convention may increase the likelihood of war or result in the escalation of an existing conflict.

important. Arms control agreements should not be destabilizing. It is counterproductive to achieve an arms control agreement that, by reducing arms, only invites attack.

Yet this is precisely what the Chemical Weapons Convention will do. The Chemical Weapons Convention is the product of a policy that equates reduced levels of armaments, in this case reduced to zero, with greater security. But the experience of World War II shows that having chemical weapons can deter a chemical attack. If the U.S. bans all of its chemical weapons, outlaw states that retain them will have a military advantage.

Almost as important as reducing the risk of war is the goal of preventing the escalation of an existing conflict to a higher level of violence. The Chemical Weapons Convention, although unintentionally, will encourage escalation in two ways. First, chemically armed enemies, knowing that the U.S. and its allies do not possess chemical weapons, will have little incentive to refrain from using such weapons. They will enjoy a unilateral advantage over the U.S., and in time of war they are likely to use it. Second, the convention may increase the likelihood that nuclear weapons will be used. Lacking chemical weapons, the U.S. will be forced to rely on nuclear weapons to deter a chemical attack on U.S. forces. While it is prudent to reserve the right to use nuclear weapons, it is certainly unwise to take steps that lower the threshold for the employment of nuclear weapons.

QUESTION #2: Are the Chemical Weapons Convention's requirements consistent with America's global responsibilities?

ANSWER #2: The Chemical Weapons Convention, by treating all nations alike, fails to acknowledge America's special role in global security.

With the Cold War over, the U.S. is the world's sole superpower. Superpower status imposes important global responsibilities which the U.S. can fulfill only by maintaining armed forces capable of projecting overwhelming force around the globe. Because America has these special responsibilities, it is treated as an exceptional case under the Nuclear Non-Proliferation Treaty.

The same principle should apply to America's chemical weapons arsenal. In Europe, Asia, the Middle East, and elsewhere, the U.S. has proved on numerous occasions that it exercises its unmatched power in a manner that is both responsible and respectful of the legitimate interests of other states. But America's global responsibilities also mean that its forces are the most likely to be engaged in major conflicts. The more dangers America faces, the greater the likelihood that chemical weapons will be used against U.S. forces.

The Chemical Weapons Convention ignores the special responsibilities of the U.S., treating all countries in the same manner. It assumes that U.S. troops face the same likelihood of chemical attack as the tiny constabulary force fielded by Costa Rica, which has the same rights and obligations under the treaty. In this way it contrasts sharply with one of the more successful arms control agreements of the post-World War II era, the Nuclear Non-Proliferation Treaty, under which the U.S. and four other nations (Britain, China, France, and Russia) are treated in a manner fundamentally different from all other nations. The Nuclear Non-Proliferation Treaty accounts for the special responsibilities and broad political roles played by these five acknowledged nuclear weapons states in world affairs. The Chemical Weapons Convention also could have done so, simply by adopting the same discriminatory approach established by the Nuclear Non-Proliferation Treaty.

QUESTION #3: Is the Chemical Weapons Convention adequately verifiable?

ANSWER #3: Despite elaborate and burdensome verification provisions, compliance with the Chemical Weapons Convention cannot be adequately verified.

The Chemical Weapons Convention is not adequately verifiable. Many lethal chemicals are common and have peaceful uses, and trying to keep track of all these chemicals throughout the world is an impossible task. In a devastating report prepared for the Defense Nuclear Agency in 1991, contractors stated: "Detecting most types of cheating [possible under the Chemical Weapons Convention] will be highly unlikely, if not impossible." This committee itself was notified of the problems with verification during a June 23, 1994, hearing. At that hearing, then-Director of Central Intelligence James Woolsey stated: "But, still, the chemical weapons problem is so difficult from an intelligence perspective that I cannot state that we have high confidence in our ability to detect noncompliance, especially on a small scale."

QUESTION #4: Are the provisions of the Chemical Weapons Convention enforceable?

ANSWER #4: Violations of the Chemical Weapons Convention are likely to go unpunished.

Verification of compliance with an arms control agreement is not enough. The U.S. also must be able to do something if other countries are caught violating the agreement.

The Chemical Weapons Convention makes only a feeble attempt to address the question of enforcement. It states that unspecified sanctions can be imposed on a state that is violating the convention, either by the Organization for the Prohibition of Chemical Weapons or by the United Nations. Ultimately, the United Nations Security Council would have to impose penalties severe enough to change the behavior of an outlaw state.

The history of the Biological Weapons Convention provides an object lesson in what can go wrong with this agreement. Starting in the early 1980s, the U.S. acknowledged that it suspected the Soviet Union of violating the Biological Weapons Convention. Yet the U.S. never lodged a complaint with the U.N. Security Council, which is charged with resolving the Biological Weapons Convention's enforcement problems just as it would under the Chemical Weapons Convention. The reason for this inaction is clear: If the U.S. had lodged a complaint against the Soviet Union, Moscow simply would have vetoed any enforcement resolution brought before the U.N. Security Council. China and Russia will have an equivalent veto authority against enforcing the provisions of the Chemical Weapons Convention as they pertain to their programs.

QUESTION #5: Does the Chemical Weapons Convention enhance U.S. national security?

ANSWER #5: By making arms control an end in itself, the Chemical Weapons Convention will not serve to protect U.S. national security.

This question establishes the most important test of arms control. Arms control is one of several means for achieving the goal of national security. It should never be thought of as an end in itself. Reduced arsenals are not always better. A comprehensive security strategy will make room for the tools of deterrence, defenses, and even offensive military operations, as well as arms control. In short, any arms control agreement must serve the supreme purpose of foreign policy, which is protecting the nation's security.

The Chemical Weapons Convention does not meet this most basic test. The convention requires that the U.S. completely abandon its chemical deterrent. But this requirement will not enhance U.S. security. Since no country is compelled

The Chemical Weapons Convention makes only a feeble attempt to address the question of enforcement.

to join the convention, it will be perfectly legal for those that do not join to retain chemical weapons. And since it is unrealistic to expect countries which want to retain chemical weapons to join, the result cannot possibly be global chemical disarmament. It makes no sense for America to give up its chemical weapons if, as a practical matter, other nations still possess them. By way of analogy, would it be in the U.S. interest to conclude a similar agreement relative to nuclear weapons? Such an agreement would require the U.S. to dispense with its nuclear arsenal even though some other countries may retain nuclear weapons. This is no longer an academic question. India, among other nations, is demanding that the U.S. commit to such an agreement in principle at the negotiations over banning nuclear tests at the Conference on Disarmament in Geneva. The precedent set by U.S. ratification of the Chemical Weapons Convention would indicate that the U.S. is willing to accept a similar agreement attempting to ban nuclear weapons.

TOWARD AN EFFECTIVE COUNTER-PROLIFERATION POLICY: THREE PRINCIPLES

The Chemical Weapons Convention is not just an arms control agreement; it is also a non-proliferation agreement. As such, it carries important implications for U.S. non-proliferation policy. While the U.S. has a clear interest in stopping the proliferation of chemical weapons around the world, an effective counter-proliferation policy cannot depend on arms control alone. A truly effective policy will balance arms control with deterrence, effective chemical defenses, and, if necessary, military options for destroying chemical weapons and weapons facilities. As the Senate considers the merits of the Chemical Weapons Convention, it should ask whether it is part of an overall counter-proliferation policy that rests on the following three principles.

PRINCIPLE #1: The need to deter a chemical attack.

Deterrence requires maintaining a credible threat to retaliate for chemical attacks against the U.S. or its allies. This retaliatory threat must be able to convince any potential aggressor that he has nothing to gain by attacking the U.S. with chemical weapons.

By requiring the destruction of chemical weapons, the Chemical Weapons Convention would deny the U.S. the capability to retaliate in kind for a chemical attack. America therefore would be left with only two options in case of a chemical attack: 1) to escalate the conflict by launching large-scale counter-attacks with conventional (non-chemical and non-nuclear) arms, or 2) to retaliate with nuclear weapons. But the Clinton Administration has not made the adjustments necessary to deal with these options. Not only is it cutting the conventional forces needed to deter chemical attacks; it also has not declared that nuclear weapons have a role in deterring chemical weapons attacks.

PRINCIPLE #2: The need for defenses against chemical weapons.

There are no guarantees, however, that deterrence will always work. Such dictators as Saddam Hussein and Muammar Qadhafi may not act rationally in a crisis or exhibit restraint. Therefore, the U.S. needs some insurance against chemical attack if deterrence fails; it needs defenses against chemical weapons and their delivery systems. U.S. forces need to be outfitted with garments, masks, and decontamination kits, and they need to be defended as well from aircraft and missiles which may carry chemical munitions.

There certainly is room for improvement in chemical defenses. The General Accounting Office's Director of Army Issues, Richard Davis, testified before Congress on April 16, 1991, that America's soldiers were neither adequately trained nor equipped to conduct operations in an environment contaminated by chemical weapons. Although some progress has been made in improving the chemical defense posture of U.S. forces during the intervening years, it is unlikely that all the vulnerabilities cited by Mr. Davis in 1991 have been eliminated. As for defenses against the delivery systems used to launch chemical attacks, the Clinton Administration has cut funding for the nation's missile defense program by more than 50 percent.

Furthermore, if history is any guide, the Chemical Weapons Convention will make it politically difficult to field better defenses. In 1969, President Nixon announced that the U.S. would forswear the use or development of biological weapons in preparation for the Biological Weapons Convention in 1972. After the Nixon decision, the U.S. biological defense program withered. This outcome was not the result of a provision in the Biological Weapons Convention outlawing defenses; it was the result of constant criticism of these programs by arms control advocates who viewed them as contrary to the spirit, although not the letter, of the Biological Weapons Convention.

The unintended consequences of the Biological Weapons Convention surfaced during the Persian Gulf War. An interim report to Congress on the results of the Gulf War stated that America's biological defense capabilities were so weak that if the Iraqis had used biological weapons, which later evidence shows they possessed, the casualty levels would have overwhelmed the military medical care system.

This same sort of vulnerability to chemical attack is likely to be the unintended consequence of the Chemical Weapons Convention. The convention does not outlaw defensive programs, yet arms control advocates are sure to lobby against defenses. The argument will go that they are not needed because chemical weapons have been banned.

PRINCIPLE #3: The need for offensive capabilities.

Defensive systems are not the sole means for countering a chemical attack. U.S. armed forces can destroy preemptively an enemy's chemical weapons and weapons facilities with air strikes and other forms of offensive combat operations. Targets for such strikes should include chemical production facilities and storage depots, as well as forces armed with chemical munitions. Destruction of the production facilities and storage depots would limit the enemy's supply of weapons, and targeting enemy forces armed with chemical munitions would lessen the chances chemical munitions will be used against U.S. and allied forces.

The Clinton Administration should be required to devise a comprehensive strategy for destroying enemy weapons and facilities in time of war.

The Clinton Administration should be required to devise a comprehensive strategy for destroying enemy weapons and facilities in time of war. It can do so by continuing and improving Pentagon programs already underway. The Air Force has conducted "sensor to shooter" experiments with the aim of devising a system for directing attacks against enemy forces within minutes of detection. The Navy has an equivalent concept called the "cooperative engagement capability." These programs need to be coordinated and focused on destroying the weapons and forces capable of delivering chemical munitions.

REDRAFTING THE CHEMICAL WEAPONS CONVENTION

The Chemical Weapons Convention is a flawed agreement. Likewise, the existing U.S. policy to counter chemical attacks also is flawed. Neither is solely the fault of the Clinton Administration. The decisions to conclude and sign the convention and to change U.S. policy toward countering chemical attacks were made by the Bush Administration.

Nevertheless, the Clinton Administration has chosen not to alter the policies begun by the Bush Administration. As the Clinton Administration proceeds down the same path, it will be up to the Senate, as it considers the Chemical Weapons Convention, to adopt a different approach. It can do so through the advice and consent process established by the United States Constitution for approving the ratification of treaties. As it does so, it should consider that:

1. A chemical weapons treaty should be modeled on the Nuclear Non-Proliferation Treaty.

Two treaties serve as models for agreements on controlling weapons of mass destruction throughout the world: the Nuclear Non-Proliferation Treaty of 1968 and the Biological Weapons Convention of 1972.

The Biological Weapons Convention is a discredited treaty. It seeks to ban biological weapons in their entirety by requiring all participating states, including the U.S., not to develop and deploy biological weapons. But it is now known that the Biological Weapons Convention was violated by the Soviet Union from the beginning. Further, a report issued by the Arms Control and Disarmament Agency on May 30, 1995, states that China, Iran, Iraq, Libya, Russia, and Taiwan either definitely have or may have violated the terms of the convention. In most of the listed cases, it is impossible to determine with absolute precision because compliance with the convention cannot be verified. Further, the report states that Egypt and Syria may have biological weapons programs. These two countries have signed but not ratified the Biological Weapons Convention. Thus, despite the evidence that other countries retained biological weapons, the U.S. has destroyed its biological deterrent.

The Nuclear Non-Proliferation Treaty, by contrast, has been relatively successful. While it has not prevented the spread of nuclear weapons, it has limited proliferation significantly. Today only a handful of countries outside the five declared nuclear states have nuclear weapons. More important, the Non-Proliferation Treaty did not require the elimination of the U.S. nuclear deterrent.

The Clinton Administration could have resolved many of the problems with the Chemical Weapons Convention by sending the treaty back to the United Nations Conference on Disarmament to be redrafted. The Administration, unfortunately, chose not to take this step. The Senate has the option of concluding that the treaty is flawed. If this conclusion were reached, the Senate could request that the Clinton Administration renegotiate the terms of the Chemical Weapons Convention so that it is modeled on the Nuclear Non-Proliferation Treaty.

If the Clinton Administration resists, there is a second alternative available to the Senate. The advice and is not limited to approving or disapproving ratification. The Senate can amend the text of a treaty. Through this amendment process, the Senate itself can redraft the Chemical Weapons Convention so that it resembles the Nuclear Non-Proliferation Treaty. Doing so would require amending the convention in several articles. After adopting these amendments, the Senate then could approve its ratification. The practical effect would be that the Clinton Administration would have to ask other treaty signatories to accept the changes made by the Senate. Thus, the net effect would be a demand to renegotiate the treaty.

2. A new policy is needed to deter chemical weapons strikes.

Changing the Chemical Weapons Convention itself, however, will not address the threat to U.S. security posed by chemical weapons. This would require changing the overall chemical weapons policy adopted by the Bush Administration. The policy established by President Bush on May 13, 1991, essentially committed the U.S. to the unconditional elimination of its chemical arsenal. This policy should be dropped, and the U.S. should state it will preserve the broadest possible array of responses to a chemical attack, including retaliation with conventional military means, an in-kind response, and, in the most extreme circumstances, a nuclear response. Further, it should not describe the specific circumstances under which it will resort to any particular response, in order to retain the greatest deterrent effect possible.

While it would be preferable that the Clinton Administration make these changes in U.S. chemical deterrence policy, the Senate also can take actions that result in the same changes. First, the Chemical Weapons Convention would have to be amended to permit a U.S. chemical deterrent. Second, the Senate could adopt a reservation—a means by which the Senate can qualify its approval of ratification—that declares that the U.S. reserves the option of retaliating against a chemical attack with nuclear weapons. It must be

The policy established by President Bush on May 13, 1991, essentially committed the U.S. to the unconditional elimination of its chemical arsenal.

acknowledged, however, that in order to adopt such a reservation the Senate may first be required to strike Article XXII of the convention. Article XXII bars reservations. Striking Article XXII is something that should be of general interest to the Senate in any event. Barring reservations narrows the freedom of action of the Senate in terms of its advice and consent role. The Senate should not accept any provisions in this convention or any future treaty that so limits its freedom of action.

3. U.S. defenses against chemical weapons need to be improved.

Pursuing an effective defense program is not prohibited by the Chemical Weapons Convention, even as currently drafted. In fact, the convention explicitly allows for the continuation of defense programs. The danger is that the implementation process will be hijacked by arms control advocates who oppose such programs and who will undermine them with calls for budget cuts.

The Senate can counter these pressures on U.S. chemical defense programs in three ways. First, it can provide adequate funding levels for chemical defense programs in the annual authorization and funding bills for the Department of Defense. But since the funding question is under the jurisdiction of other Senate committees, the Foreign Relations Committee may prefer to focus on establishing clearly defined standards for the military in terms chemical defense preparedness. A condition could be attached to the resolution of ratification that requires the Secretary of Defense to certify that the Department of Defense has met the requirements for improving chemical defense preparedness made by Richard Davis of the General Accounting Office in testimony before Congress. These include meeting minimum chemical training standards set forth in service regulations and properly integrating chemical defense training into the overall training program for U.S. troops.

The Senate should also set requirements for improving U.S. defenses against delivery vehicles used to launch chemical attacks, particularly ballistic missiles. This must include a requirement for the development and deployment of missile defenses capable of effectively destroying chemically armed ballistic missiles in the boost phase. The Senate could force this outcome by adopting a condition requiring the Administration to propose such a boost-phase defense for deployment by a specific date.

4. The U.S. capability to destroy chemical weapons production and storage facilities, as well as deployed forces with chemical weapons, should be improved.

Defensive systems cannot meet all the requirements for defending U.S. and allied forces and civilians against chemical attack. These can be met only by maintaining offensive capabilities for striking at enemy positions. For example, countering enemy artillery firing chemical munitions requires an offensive response with opposing artillery or air strikes, as does interrupting enemy command and control networks and destroying chemical production and supply facilities.

The U.S. proved during the Persian Gulf War that it has an effective deep strike capability. Many command and control centers, for example, were destroyed by U.S. air power in and around Baghdad. But this is not to say that improvements cannot be made. For example, the U.S. had trouble countering Iraqi mobile Scud missiles with air power. To deal with this problem, the military services, and the Air Force and Navy in particular, have launched programs which are focused on enhancing the U.S. ability to strike quickly and accurately at enemy forces and facilities. The Senate should direct the Department of Defense to coordinate these programs and focus them on countering weapons of mass destruction and their delivery systems, including chemical weapons. The Senate again has the option of adopting a condition during its advice and consent process that forces the Clinton Administration to continue these programs and gear them to meeting the weapons of mass destruction threat.

5. The Chemical Weapons Convention's arms control enforcement mechanisms need to be strengthened.

There are three problems with U.S. policy for enforcing compliance with the Chemical Weapons Convention. First, the Chemical Weapons Convention has a built-in conflict of interest in terms of enforcement. By establishing the U.N. Security Council as the court of last appeal in its enforcement process, the convention will allow the U.N. Security Council's five permanent members to veto any pending resolution ordering sanctions against it for an alleged violation. Any attempt to impose sanctions—on China, for example—for violating the convention are doomed to failure at the outset.

This problem can be resolved by redrafting the Chemical Weapons Convention along the lines of the Nuclear Non-Proliferation Treaty. Since the redrafted convention would establish declared chemical weapons states, it would be logical that these states be the five permanent members of the U.N. Security Council, thereby eliminating the conflict of interest.

The second enforcement problem is that the U.S. historically has been reluctant to take action to remedy a violation by an arms control treaty partner. Despite clear evidence of Soviet violations of the Biological Weapons Convention and the 1972 Anti-Ballistic Missile Treaty, the U.S. did not take the proportionate steps allowed to it under international law. Thus, the violations went unpunished.

Meeting the chemical weapons threat requires redrafting the Chemical Weapons Convention to declare that a few countries, including the U.S., are weapons states.

Solving this problem will require a change in the government process for handling these issues. Currently, the Arms Control and Disarmament Agency reports annually on arms control treaty violations, but there is no requirement for follow-up. Ultimately, the law could be changed to require that the President propose a proportionate response to a reported treaty violation no later than 60 days after the report is issued. This would guarantee a substantive response once a violation is discovered.

The third problem is addressing the actions of states that refuse to ratify or accede to the Chemical Weapons Convention. This can be dealt with only by retaining a strong military posture that can deter and, if necessary, retaliate against a chemical attack. This is the ultimate insurance policy, but it can be maintained over the long term only by the actions of a Congress determined to fund and supervise America's defense programs.

CONCLUSION

Meeting the chemical weapons threat requires redrafting the Chemical Weapons Convention to declare that a few countries, including the U.S., are weapons states. It also requires a policy under which the U.S. reserves the right and capability to respond to chemical attack either in kind or with nuclear weapons, in addition to conventional means.

Perhaps the best example in history of a successful deterrence policy came during World War II. Despite the existence of chemical arsenals, chemical weapons were not used widely during that conflict. The reason: The Allied powers, including the United States, convinced the Axis that the use of such weapons would result in swift retaliation.

The U.S. may now be throwing away this successful policy. By adopting the Chemical Weapons Convention and declaring a unilateral policy of neither maintaining nor using chemical weapons, even in retaliation, the U.S. would eliminate its chemical deterrent even though it could never be sure that potential enemies have taken equivalent steps. U.S. national security interests demand that this process be reversed. The U.S. must not abandon its ability to deter attacks with chemical weapons.

Chemical Reaction[2]

It would seem an indisputable good: a treaty to eliminate poison gas from Beijing to Buenos Aires. Yet the new Chemical Weapons Convention is having trouble in the Senate. And the more the treaty is debated, the deeper the trouble. In congressional hearings and public forums, even the treaty's champions have been forced to concede our severely limited ability to monitor compliance and enforce the ban.

As a result, the chief pro-treaty argument is no longer that the CWC, as the treaty is acronymically known, will abolish chemical weapons—for it obviously will not—but that the CWC is better than nothing. Administration officials, in their standard pitch to skeptical senators, now stress that the treaty is on balance worthwhile, if flawed, and rebuke critics for measuring the treaty against an unrealistic standard of "perfection." "The limits imposed by the CWC surely are imperfect," former National Security Adviser Brent Scowcroft and former CIA Director John Deutch contended in a recent *Washington Post* op-ed, "but . . . it is hard to see how its imperfect constraints are worse than no constraints at all."

It would seem an indisputable good: a treaty to eliminate poison gas from Beijing to Buenos Aires.

The it's-better-than-nothing argument has some potency. After all, no decent person wants poison gas to proliferate. Conservatives and liberals alike want to continue to destroy the entire U.S. chemical arsenal regardless of what happens to the CWC. So even a small step in the direction of global abolition would be valuable. But the treaty is not such a step. It is not better than nothing. Indeed, it would eliminate export controls that now impede rogue states from developing their chemical warfare capabilities. And, as many senators have discovered after examining the treaty's 186-page text, it would exacerbate the problem of poison gas proliferation around the world.

Article XI, for instance, states that parties to the treaty shall:

> Not maintain among themselves any restrictions, including those in any international agreements, incompatible with the obligations undertaken under this Convention, which would restrict or impede trade and the development and promotion of scientific and technological knowledge in the field of

2. Article by Douglas J. Feith for the *New Republic* p12 Mar. 24, 1997. Copyright © 1997 the New Republic. Reprinted with permission.

chemistry for industrial, agricultural, research, medical, pharmaceutical or other peaceful purposes.

What this means is that the United States must not restrict chemical trade with any other CWC party—even Iran and Cuba, both of which are CWC signatories. Similarly, CWC Article X obliges countries to share with other parties technology relating to chemical weapons defense. "Each State Party," the article says, "undertakes to facilitate, and shall have the right to participate in, the fullest possible exchange of equipment, material and scientific and technological information concerning means of protection against chemical weapons."

Once Iran and Cuba ratify the treaty, our current export controls against them will surely be attacked as impermissible. Furthermore, those countries, upon joining the CWC, will claim entitlement to the advanced countries' "scientific and technological information" on how to protect their armed forces against chemical weapons. A crucial element of an offensive chemical weapons capability is the means to protect one's own forces from the weapons' effects.

Even if the U.S. government decides to maintain export controls against Iran and Cuba, Articles X and XI will invite other countries to transfer dangerous technology to them. Germany can be expected to invoke the treaty against any U.S. official who protests a planned sale of a chemical factory to, say, Iran. Indeed, Bonn could not only argue that its firms are allowed to sell chemical technology to Iran, but that they are actually obliged to do so, for Iran will have renounced chemical weapons by joining the CWC.

Articles X and XI are modeled on similar provisions in the Nuclear Non-Proliferation Treaty, called "atoms for peace," which even admirers acknowledge have spread the very nuclear technology the treaty was intended to contain. When Iran, Iraq and North Korea became signatories, they quickly gained access to this sensitive technology, ostensibly "for peaceful purposes." Yet it helped these outlaw states to develop their nuclear weapons programs. The CWC encourages the same abuse. Even Scowcroft and Deutch acknowledge "we must ensure that the CWC is not exploited to facilitate the diffusion of CWC specific technology ... even to signatory states." Alas, the perverse product of the CWC will be "poisons for peace."

Without the treaty, any country that wants to destroy its chemical weapons can do so, as is the United States. But, for the sake of declaring an unenforceable ban on chemical weapons possession, the CWC will undermine existing export controls that are, in fact, doing some good. It is a stunning, though not unprecedented, example of arms control diplomacy resulting in the opposite of its intended effect. The treaty brings to mind Santayana's definition of a "fanatic" as someone who redoubles his effort upon losing sight of his goal. As this absurdity impresses itself upon the Senate, that body appears intent on rejecting the agreement, thereby sending the administration and the world a beneficial message: arms control treaties should make us more secure, not less. [On April 24, 1997, the U.S. Senate ratified the CWC.]

Without the treaty, any country that wants to destroy its chemical weapons can do so, as is the United States.

Stay the Course on Chemical Weapons Ban[3]

Leave it to Washington to toil for more than two decades to create a new arms control regime that abolishes poison gas and then, once it takes off, to begin foolishly undercutting its own achievement by trying to water down the treaty's verification provisions. But that is exactly what Congress is trying to do and it must be dissuaded.

On April 29, 1997, a revolution unlike any other in arms control history began. Teams of inspectors began criss-crossing the globe to monitor compliance with the Chemical Weapons Convention (CWC), which bans the development, production, stockpiling, transfer, and use of poison gas. Participating countries are obligated to destroy their chemical arsenals and weapons production facilities under international supervision. In addition, inspectors will routinely check the activities of the chemical industry to ensure that chemicals used in commercial products are not being diverted to produce lethal chemical agents.

Perhaps the most notable achievement of the CWC's early days is that so many governments embraced a treaty that unambiguously mandates the acceptance of short-notice challenge inspections of any site on their territory suspected of engaging in prohibited activity. To date, more than 100 countries have joined this accord, and more than 60 others have signed but not yet ratified it. The possessors of the world's two largest chemical weapons stockpiles, Russia and the United States, are CWC members, and the roster of participants includes countries from every corner of the earth—South Africa, Cuba, Brazil, Japan, France, Jordan, and Belarus, to name a few.

Of the roughly two dozen countries considered likely to possess a chemical weapons capability, only North Korea, Syria, Egypt, Iraq, and Libya remain outside the CWC. In May 2000, the CWC's automatic economic penalties will cut off aspiring proliferators from the marketplace of commercial chemicals that can also have military utility. Whether by making it more difficult for countries to stockpile poison gas or by compelling countries to relinquish their chemical

3. Article by Amy E. Smithson from *Issues in Science and Technology* p37-40 Winter 1997-98. Copyright © 1998 by the University of Texas at Dallas, Richardson, TX.

weapons programs, the CWC endeavors to reverse the proliferation trend.

U.S. INTERESTS UNDERCUT

The CWC undoubtedly would have been seriously undermined without U.S. participation. At the eleventh hour and after a rancorous debate, the U.S. Senate voted to ratify the CWC on April 24, just five days before it was activated. Even before ratification, the United States had already begun to destroy its stockpile of more than 29,000 metric tons of poison gas. CWC inspectors have initiated continuous monitoring operations at the destruction plants at Johnston Atoll in the Pacific Ocean and at Tooele, Utah. Destruction facilities will be constructed at seven other locations where U.S. chemical weapons are stored. In addition, inspections have been conducted at former U.S. chemical weapons facilities and at the sites involved in the U.S. chemical weapons defense program. The treaty permits research to develop and test protective gear, vaccines, and antidotes, but will closely watch defense programs. Thus, CWC inspectors are monitoring all aspects of the United States' former chemical weapons program.

Congress has tried to tinker with the CWC's verification provisions to give U.S. facilities a break on the treaty's stringent monitoring provisions.

Nonetheless, the United States is not in full compliance with the CWC because it has not yet approved its implementing legislation. As a result, the U.S. chemical industry, which supported the CWC's ratification and has accepted the treaty's data reporting and inspection burdens, does not have the guidelines to fulfill these obligations. The legislation directs the chemical industry to provide data about certain chemicals that the CWC's inspectors would then check during routine inspections. Both houses of Congress passed the implementing legislation, but the Senate did not vote on a rider that the House attached just before Congress recessed. Thus, the legislation died.

Perhaps equally disturbing, Congress has tried to tinker with the CWC's verification provisions to give U.S. facilities a break on the treaty's stringent monitoring provisions. In the implementing legislation, both the House and the Senate passed language that would allow the president to refuse a challenge inspection on the grounds that it could threaten U.S. security. This language directly contradicts the obligation that the United States undertook when it joined the treaty to accept challenge inspections at any time, at any place on U.S. territory. The Senate also stipulated when ratifying the CWC that no samples collected during a routine or challenge inspection may be taken out of the country for additional analysis. Since the inspectors will carry analytical equipment with them, they will rarely invoke the right to conduct off-site analysis. When they do, however, detailed analysis at laboratories certified by the CWC's inspectorate in the Hague may be crucial to clarifying whether a country has cheated.

The Pentagon, the intelligence community, and the chemical industry have all agreed to the CWC's verification measures, but some members of Congress continue to object based on false concerns that the very inspection measures needed to verify compliance abroad will compromise national security or confidential business information at home. What these members fail to appreciate is that the CWC contains ample protections to safeguard such information, which is why the chemical industry, the Pentagon, and the intelligence community gave the CWC their seal of approval. When Congress reconvenes, it may continue trying to create exemptions in the CWC's verification regime. If Congress does so, then other countries will surely exploit these loopholes. In short, U.S.-made exclusions to the CWC's verification regime will ultimately backfire on U.S. security interests when other countries deny a U.S. challenge inspection request or thwart inspectors' efforts to have a sample analyzed off-site. Such an outcome would gut the treaty's verification protocol.

EVIDENCE OF THE CWC'S CLOUT

Poison gas has long been so universally abhorred that governments have been loath to admit having stockpiled weapons or built facilities to make chemical agents. Before the CWC went into effect, Russia and the United States were the only two countries to admit possessing chemical weapons, even though intelligence agencies had concluded that about two dozen countries had chemical weapons programs.

Russia, which has declared that it possesses some 40,000 metric tons of chemical weapons, ratified the CWC in November 1997. Strapped for funds to destroy its arsenal, Moscow is banking on the willingness of other countries to help pay for its destruction program. Likely donor countries, however, may withhold significant contributions until the CWC's inspections settle concerns that in the late 1980s and early 1990s the Soviet, now Russian, chemical weapons complex developed, tested, and produced small quantities of an entirely new generation of deadly nerve agents. Moscow has denied that this activity occurred. Further, Russia wants to exempt from inspection former chemical weapons production facilities that have already been converted to peaceful enterprises. Other countries that are in full compliance with the treaty will insist that Russia divulge all required data and allow unimpeded access to treaty-relevant sites. Only full cooperation with the CWC's inspectorate will garner continued Western aid for Russia's chemical weapons destruction program.

Now that the CWC has strengthened the behavioral norm against chemical weapons, more countries are terminating their chemical weapons programs. China declared having former chemical weapons production facilities, which CWC inspectors have already visited and mothballed. India said that it possessed production facilities, along with an arsenal of as-yet-unknown size. Pakistan and Iran, both suspected of harboring chemical weapons programs, joined the treaty in November 1997 and are scheduled to declare what they possess early in 1998. France acknowledged that it had production facilities. In addition, one more nation has reported to the CWC inspectorate that it has a chemical weapons stockpile, but that country has not announced this to the public.

By the end of October, the CWC's inspectors had completed more than 85 inspections in 20 member states. Among the sites inspected were 34 chemical weapons production facilities, 19 chemical weapons storage facilities, and 23 facilities that produce small quantities of highly toxic chemicals for permitted purposes, such as defensive or medical research. Five chemical weapons destruction facilities are being continuously monitored. When the numbers are tallied, the CWC's potential to reduce the chemical weapons threat becomes apparent: Within six months of the CWC's activation, more than 80 facilities involved in chemical weapons-related activities had already received the scrutiny of international inspectors. Although there were high hopes for the CWC, few thought so much would be accomplished so quickly.

As might be expected with the startup of a system of international legal requirements and a new inspection agency, all of the news is not so encouraging. For example, countries have dallied in providing their assessed contributions to the inspectorate. The funding shortfall was so severe during the

Within six months of the CWC's activation, more than 80 facilities involved in chemical weapons-related activities had already received the scrutiny of international inspectors.

summer of 1997, when the United States and Japan were withholding funds, that the inspectorate's director, Jose Bustani of Brazil, notified participating states that he would soon have to halt inspections. The financial situation has improved somewhat but is still a major concern.

Another problem frustrating the inspectorate has been the failure of participating countries to file declarations. Roughly 30 of the more than 100 member countries have not met the CWC's initial paperwork requirements, and some of the declarations received were incomplete. To a certain extent, this problem was predictable. Unlike the United States and Russia, the lion's share of the CWC's members lack extensive experience in handling declarations or inspections. With time, the responsible authorities in the CWC member states will become more accustomed to the treaty's requirements, and the track record in this area will improve.

A different type of tug-of-war brewing in the Hague pertains to the CWC's secrecy rules. Under the treaty, a government can require the inspectorate to protect the confidentiality of all information in its declarations and inspections. Although some details should be held in the tightest secrecy, a certain level of transparency is needed to promote awareness of and confidence in the CWC. Some CWC members are extremely reluctant to release information about treaty-related activities that have reversed longstanding denials about the existence of chemical weapons programs. Bustani has managed to persuade some countries to allow him to divulge broad characterizations about CWC implementation activities. However, more information needs to be publicly presented. Sensitivities about the release of treaty-related data should ease as governments gain confidence that monitoring activities confirm their compliance with the CWC and allow them to be members in good standing of the international community.

If governments can overcome the initial discomfort caused by the managed transparency of the CWC's intrusive verification provisions, they will grow to appreciate how the treaty can enhance their security. No longer will decisionmakers in one capital question whether a neighboring country is mounting a clandestine chemical weapons program; inspectors will routinely visit high-risk facilities in all participating states, and challenge inspection rights can be exercised to confirm or allay suspicions. This type of cooperative security

Roughly 30 of the more than 100 member countries have not met the CWC's initial paperwork requirements, and some of the declarations received were incomplete.

arrangement is far preferable to the uncertainties that lead to the expense and instability of arms races.

Should the CWC continue on its current successful course and participating states resolve the shortcomings that have hindered the treaty's implementation thus far, the CWC may well become a strong model for future cooperative security and disarmament arrangements. Diplomats negotiating a verification protocol to strengthen the Biological and Toxin Weapons Convention, which lacks any monitoring provisions, are already considering patterning verification measures for this accord after those contained in the CWC.

Consequently, the United States needs to provide leadership to ensure the full and effective implementation of the CWC, at home as well as abroad. It must not create loopholes in the treaty it labored so long to achieve. The CWC's model of managed cooperative security is one that clearly serves longterm U.S. security interests and deserves unwavering support from Washington.

Ratify the Chemical Weapons Convention[4]

International agreements prohibiting chemical weapons began in the 17th century, when the Germans and French agreed to prohibit poison bullets. New chemical toxins and new ways to deliver them have kept treaties to ban such weapons of mass destruction on the diplomatic and security agendas of large and small nations ever since. Although chemical weapons are among the most deadly military devices (the World War I battles in which they were used caused 8% of the deaths), never have they achieved eventual victory, and the Geneva Protocol of the 1920s sought to ban their use. The Chemical Weapons Convention (CWC) is the latest and best attempt at ridding the world of chemical weapons by targeting both their possession and the means to produce them. Only if the major powers agree to participate and to enforce its provisions without hesitation will the CWC increase the national security of all states by reducing the threat from chemical warfare. An excellent overview of the main issues can be seen at the World Wide Web site of the Provisional Technical Secretariat of the Preparatory Commission for the Organisation for the Prohibition of Chemical Weapons (http://www.opcw.nlguide.htm), along with a list of countries that have become signatory parties to the CWC.

The CWC has now been signed by the leaders of 161 nations and will become effective on 29 April 1997. Under the Reagan and Bush administrations, the United States was instrumental in negotiating this agreement, and George Bush signed it in 1991. However, as of this writing, the U.S. Senate has still not ratified that signing. Unless that step is taken, the United States will find itself in the company of states that intend to ignore the convention, such as Iran, Libya, and North Korea.

Nonparticipation has diplomatic, economic, and scientific consequences. Nonratification does not give us a seat at the table with our allies, almost all of whom have ratified, and provides an excuse to other nonmember countries to remain outside. Only ratifying nations may join the Executive Council (which will prepare for implementation of the provisions

Only if the major powers agree to participate and to enforce its provisions without hesitation will the CWC increase the national security of all states by reducing the threat from chemical warfare.

---

4. Article by Floyd E. Bloom from *Science* p179 Apr. 11, 1997. Copyright © 1997 American Association for the Advancement of Science. Reprinted with permission.

of the treaty) or the Technical Secretariat (which will, among other functions, provide inspectors for suspected stockpiles or production sites and monitor the destruction of existing stocks). Failure to ratify the CWC will constrain some aspects of chemical trade with international partners who are member states. The consequences of these restrictions will affect chemicals required in research throughout the scientific community, as well as major domestic industries in agriculture, textiles, pharmaceuticals, and transportation The CWC will not alter U.S. policy on chemical weapons: The United States has already begun destroying its aging stockpile of chemical agents and expects to complete the process by 2004; no new chemical weapons are planned.

Nevertheless, U.S. ratification has been stalled in the Senate for more than 2 years. Politics aside, the CWC has been opposed by groups who believe that compliance with its provisions will be unverifiable (small amounts of highly toxic chemicals or their precursors could be undetectable) and unenforceable (all penalties for violations would require approval by the Security Council of the United Nations). However, the need for improved means of remote sampling and for enhanced sensitivity in chemical identification and detection would surely benefit from U.S. expertise and instrumentadon development in these fields. Opponents of the CWC also fear that any international inspection of chemical facilities could result in theft of proprietary processes that now give U.S. chemical manufacturers their edge. No group would have more to fear from this pillage than the U.S. chemical industry, yet the Chemical Manufacturers Association, along with the American Chemical Society, have been strong proponents of the CWC.

In February 1997, the AAAS Board urged every member of the Senate to ratify the CWC. The Senate should consider stipulations that will make the CWC effective not only for U.S. security but for world security. Not only must the U.S. Senate vote for ratification without further delay, the United States must use its diplomatic influence to persuade other present nonsignatories—especially Russia, China, and Iran—to ratify the CWC as responsible members of the global community. Science urges its U.S. readers to make their feelings known to the Senate and asks its international readers to support the CWC locally.

Japan and China: Cleansing Job[5]

When the Japanese army retreated from China at the end of the Second World War, it left behind thousands of shells filled with deadly chemicals. Half a century on, Japan faces the huge cost of disposing of these rusting relics of its military past. Starting on April 29th, the countries that have ratified the Chemical Weapons Convention have ten years in which to get rid of their stocks of chemicals used in warfare, to dismantle the plants for making them, and to remove any chemical weapons left behind in other countries. Japan's sole obligation is to deal with the shells left in China in 1945. That is more than enough to keep the Japanese busy.

China has not yet ratified the convention it signed with 129 other countries in Paris in 1993, but since 1991 it has been negotiating with Japan on the best way to clear up the old chemical dumps. Most of the dumps are in Jilin province, in north-east China. This is part of Manchuria, which Japan invaded in 1931, creating a puppet state. Surveys by China in the 1950s put the number of chemical shells left by Japan at 2m, mostly in the Harbin district. Smaller caches of chemical weapons have been found elsewhere in China.

They are a continual danger. Claims for damages are working their way through the Tokyo courts on behalf of Chinese injured or killed by accidentally coming into contact with the chemicals. Officials in Beijing say that more than 2,000 people have been hurt or killed in this way.

Japan has sent seven teams to various parts of China to examine the chemical dumps. The Japanese government puts the number of its chemical shells in China at 700,000, rather than the 2m estimated by the Chinese. The Japanese researchers say they have found no evidence that they contaminated the land or affected the health of local people.

The Chinese have reluctantly agreed to let the Japanese deal with the crumbling shells in China rather than cart them back to Japan. But it will cost the Japanese government dearly. In March last year, Japan's prime minister, Ryutaro Hashimoto, promised his Chinese counterpart, Li Peng, that Japan would respond to the Chemical Weapons Convention "with sincerity"—in other words, foot the bill.

When the Japanese army retreated from China at the end of the Second World War, it left behind thousands of shells filled with deadly chemicals.

---

5. Article from the *Economist* p36-7 Apr. 5, 1997. Copyright © 1997 the Economist Newspaper Group, Inc. Reprinted with permission. Further reproduction prohibited. www.economist.com.

Japan had hoped to get away with simply building a factory ship that would process the poisonous gases and toxic chemicals in a Chinese port and float away when the job was done. But in December it agreed instead to build a special processing plant in Jilin province. The site and the technology to be used are expected to be decided soon. The cost of the plant is put at up to ¥500 billion ($4.1 billion).

Neither China nor Japan has any experience of disposing of old chemical weapons. Japanese technicians have been sent to Germany, Britain and America to study various ways of handling the shells. The Germans have become particularly adept at clearing stocks of chemical weapons left over from the first and second world wars. But, at most, they have had to dispose of no more than 30 shells a day. To meet the chemical convention's ten-year plan, the Japanese plant in China will have to process upwards of 200 a day.

IV. Terrorism at Home and Abroad

Editor's Introduction

With biological and chemical weapons technology becoming cheaper and easier to develop in recent years, there has been concern over such capabilities being used by terrorists. While nuclear weapons are well beyond the reach of most terrorist groups due to the advanced technology and high costs involved, biological and chemical weapons have quite literally become the "poor man's weapons of mass destruction." For the first time in modern history, it is conceivable that independent individuals can wage war with nations using such means. In 1995, a terrorist group exposed commuters on a Tokyo train to deadly sarin nerve gas, killing 12. Incidents such as this have demonstrated that there are terrorist groups both able and willing to launch biological/chemical attacks, and these incidents only hint at what such groups may be capable of. The U.S. in particular is faced not only with extremist factions based on foreign soil, but with the ever-growing presence of militant, anti-government groups within our own borders.

President Clinton recently addressed the issue of chemical and germ attacks by terrorists. In "Clinton Describes Terrorism Threat for 21st Century," Judith Miller and William J. Broad of the *New York Times* report on the president's statements, in which he deems it very probable that the United States will at least be threatened with a serious attack in the near future. Clinton also explains that any terrorist activity would be met with a swift and appropriate response. Even more than chemical weapons, Clinton expresses deep concern over the danger of biological agents, which have a much longer-lasting impact due to their communicative nature.

"Terrorism's New Theater," originally published in *Insight*, takes a penetrating look at the chemical and biological warfare capabilities of terrorists. Author Tiffany Danitz illustrates the wide availability and relatively low cost of potentially lethal substances, biological agents in particular. How such an attack could be perpetrated is discussed as well. Danitz also mentions the U.S. Defense Department's inoculation of soldiers against anthrax, pointing out that there are no plans for similar measures involving civilians, despite the possibility of terrorist strikes at home.

"Germ Warfare in 'Jew York'" addresses the presence of ultra-right wing racist factions within the United States. Larry Wayne Harris, arrested in Las Vegas in 1995 for possession of anthrax, is believed to belong to one such group, many of which consider places such as New York to be primary targets for chemical/bacteriological attack due to the mix of ethnicities and races which make up their populations. Writing for the *Village Voice*, James Ridgeway provides some background into Harris's past, and gives significant evidence for the biological and chemical warfare capabilities of terrorist groups within the country.

The arrest of Larry Wayne Harris is also the subject of "Arrests Reveal Threat of Biological Weapons," a report by Andrew C. Revkin for the *New York Times*. Revkin evaluates the federal government's investigation of Harris and his confiscated substances. There is also a comparison made to earlier incidents, such as the terrorist attack in a Japanese subway in which nerve gas was actually used. The government's response to such an alarming discovery of deadly germ agents inside the U.S. is discussed, with Revkin pointing out how the Harris arrest emphasizes the need for greater watchfulness.

The final piece in this chapter is an extensive essay from the journal *Comparative Strategy* entitled "Terrorism, Technology, and the Socioeconomics of Death." This article takes a very unique look at the biological warfare capabilities of terrorists, discussing it from a pragmatic, economic point of view. Author Martin Shubik writes in depth about the economic ramifications of this "new warfare," and how it grants relatively small groups of civilians the kinds of war-waging powers once reserved only for nation-states. The cheapness of biological weapons is offered by Shubik as the main reason for this shift. One of the more fascinating elements of this essay is the way in which the author compares different modes of terrorist activity over the centuries, culminating in today's era of bio-terrorists.

Clinton Describes Terrorism Threat for 21st Century[1]

WASHINGTON—President Clinton said Thursday that it is "highly likely" that a terrorist group will launch or threaten a germ or chemical attack on American soil within the next few years.

In an interview in the Oval Office late in the day, Clinton said he had been persuaded by intelligence reports that the United States needs to bolster its defenses.

"I want to raise public awareness of this," the President said in the 45-minute interview, "without throwing people into an unnecessary panic."

He said he wanted Americans "not to be afraid or asleep. I think that's the trick."

Without providing specifics, Clinton warned that any attack with germ or chemical weapons would prompt "at least a proportionate if not a disproportionate response." The United States has signed treaties not to use chemical or germ weapons.

He made the assertions as the White House disclosed that the Administration planned to ask Congress for $2.8 billion in the next budget year to fight terrorists armed with such unconventional weapons as deadly germs, chemicals and electronic devices. Clinton insisted during the interview that his drive to expand the budget for these programs was rooted in the growing danger of such threats.

Elaborating on some of the initiatives he intends to unveil on Friday, Clinton said he is weighing a proposal from the Defense Department to establish a commander in chief for the defense of the continental United States, a step that civil liberties groups strongly resist.

Such a step would go far beyond the civil defense measures and bomb shelters that marked the cold war, setting up instead a military leadership to help fight chaos and disarray if an attack occurred. The Pentagon has commanders overseeing regions around the globe, but none for the continental United States.

Critics fear such moves could open the door to rising military influence and a loss of individual rights, but Clinton

Without providing specifics, Clinton warned that any attack with germ or chemical weapons would prompt "at least a proportionate if not a disproportionate response."

---

1. Article by Judith Miller and William J. Broad for the *New York Times* Jan. 22, 1999. Copyright © 1999 the New York Times Company. Reprinted with permission.

insisted that such erosions would never occur, even while acknowledging the danger.

"We've got to preserve civil liberties, resolve all doubt in favor of that, and if there's a question, bring it to me," Clinton said, while acknowledging there were specific concerns in areas like computer security. He did not offer details on how he would insure protection.

The President gave the interview as his lawyers ended their defense presentation at his impeachment trial in the Senate. Since the Monica S. Lewinsky issue surfaced a year ago today, the President has given almost no interviews to major American news organizations.

At the very end of the interview, he answered one question related to impeachment by agreeing that the impeachment ordeal had placed a great strain on his family and by expressing the hope that the worst was over.

Despite the political pressures, Clinton appeared relaxed and deeply engaged in the complex scientific and policy issues raised by what the White House has called 21st-century threats. He smiled repeatedly, yet spoke of sleepless nights pondering new security challenges.

In the interview, Clinton said he hoped that a major legacy of his Presidency would be to stave off unconventional attacks. He said he would be delighted if, decades later, Americans looked back on any such threat as "the dog that didn't bark."

Among other new considerations, Clinton said he was weighing a proposal to give anthrax vaccinations to police, fire, public health and other emergency officials in cities throughout the country. That would be in addition to the current drive to vaccinate more than two million soldiers.

He declined to say whether he himself had been vaccinated against deadly germ agents, saying that the Secret Service had advised him to remain silent.

He also vowed to forge ahead despite Congressional criticism with cooperative programs with Russia aimed at providing jobs to 8,000 former weapons scientists who might otherwise be tempted to work with rogue states or terrorist groups.

Among the programs he will highlight on Friday are developing new vaccines, stockpiling antibiotics, setting up emergency medical teams in major cities and a corps of computer experts who could respond quickly to electronic attacks.

[Clinton] said he would be delighted if, decades later, Americans looked back on any such threat as "the dog that didn't bark."

With his Presidency under fire, it is unclear how much of the proposed $2.8 billion in military funds and programs Clinton will be able to get through the Republican-dominated Congress. But lawmakers have usually supported White House efforts to fight terrorism.

Clinton said that of all the new threats, the one that "keeps me awake at night" is the possibility of germ attack. "A chemical attack would be horrible, but it would be finite," he said, adding that it would not spread. But a biological attack could spread, he added, "kind of like the gift that keeps on giving."

Clinton said he had begun worrying about biological terrorism and other unconventional threats six years ago, in February 1993, after Islamic radicals exploded a bomb under the World Trade Center in New York. The bombing one month after he came into office killed six people and injured more than a thousand.

He said his concerns about the danger of germ or chemical attack were deepened by the Oklahoma City bombing, terrorist attacks in the Middle East and Africa on American embassies and facilities, and reports that Iraq had retained chemical weapons it claimed to have destroyed. Clinton said he was also troubled by the activities of a Japanese cult, Aum Shinrikyo, which attacked the Tokyo subway system in 1995 with a nerve agent, killing 12 and injuring 5,000.

He said on Thursday that terrorists were probably a greater danger than rogue states, which would be afraid to openly attack American targets for fear of retaliation.

He noted that Osama bin Laden, a Saudi fugitive who is accused of masterminding the United States Embassy bombings in Africa in August, has "made an effort to get chemical weapons" and "may have" tried to get germ weapons. "We don't know that they have them," Clinton said.

Clinton asserted that "a lot of what we've done already," some of it secret, "has delayed" foreign efforts to develop and deploy chemical, biological or nuclear weapons.

He said that ultimately, America's best defense against unconventional warfare and bioterrorism in particular would be scientific strides in deciphering the genetic material in microbes and humans, so that vaccines could be tailored for quick response to an attack.

This, he said, would allow defense to stay ahead of the offense. His hope, he said, was that America would use "each new wave of technology to close the gap between offense and defense."

He specifically endorsed the Human Genome Project, a costly federally financed effort to map out human genetic material, saying it would be an important part of the defensive shield his Administration is building.

Clinton's personal interest in the threat, aides agree, has become a powerful force behind a series of secret Federal meetings, actions and directives meant to bolster the nation's anti-terrorism work and to counter what they describe as a growing danger to civilians.

The new budget outlined by the White House today and to be formally unveiled Friday by Clinton includes a total of $10 billion to defend against terrorism, weapons of mass destruction, and cyber attacks, according to a White House statement.

Most of the money—about $8.5 billion—is earmarked for efforts to defend American embassies and other United States buildings and personnel against conventional weapons such as car and truck bombs. The rest, or about $2.8 billion, is divided among existing and a few new programs to counter biological, chemical, and computer attacks, especially those that would cripple key parts of the Government or the economy.

Clinton insisted in the interview Thursday that such money would be "well spent," despite detractors and skeptics of the new exotic threats.

"And if there is never an incident, nobody would be happier than me 20 years from now if the same critics would be able to say, 'Oh, see, Clinton was a kook, nothing happened.' I would be the happiest man on earth."

About $2.8 billion is divided among existing and a few new programs to counter biological chemical, and computer attacks.

Terrorism's New Theater[2]

The specter of biological warfare has led the Defense Department to inoculate 2 million U.S. soldiers against anthrax. Civilians, however, will remain at risk.

Just as the ice was beginning to crack under the strain of the April sun in 1979, scores of residents in the Russian town of Sverdlovsk were struck down by a deadly virus. An explosion at a nearby illegal germ warfare station belched a cloud of anthrax over the Ural Mountain city. Spores rained down on the residents, sending thousands to hospitals complaining of flulike symptoms; within five days most were dead. The Soviet Union had promised not to develop, produce or stockpile bacteriological agents and weapons with its signature on the Biological Weapons Convention, or BWC treaty of 1975. Since then other rogue states and roving terrorists have managed to weaponize and produce several biological agents, including anthrax and human plague.

"The threat is now out there, front and center, and we have to prepare for a new and more dangerous era of terrorism" as we enter the new century, says Jeffrey Simon, director of the Political Risk Assessment Co., a consulting firm specializing in security and terrorism research, in Santa Monica, Calif.

Armed with the advantage of efficient, economical, mass-killing capabilities, any nation or terrorist can raise the stakes considerably in a world in which little preparation has been taken against such attacks. Any group with access to reasonably advanced pharmaceutical and medical facilities has the capacity to build biological weapons. The disadvantages they face are few: limited life spans of the organisms, loss of a percentage of the agent in an explosion and a stigma much worse than that experienced by Oklahoma City bomber Timothy McVeigh.

Says Simon: "We are having to start from scratch in terms of anticipating terrorist targets or groups who may use biological or chemical terrorism because the tactics and the targets will not necessarily be the same as we have seen in conventional terrorism."

But, for groups that have a doomsday mentality and little need to develop or satisfy a supportive constituency, these

Any group with access to reasonably advanced pharmaceutical and medical facilities has the capacity to build biological weapons.

---

weapons are choice. The Aum Shinrikyo, or Sacred Truth cult in Japan killed 12 passengers in the Tokyo subway system with sarin nerve gas in 1995. But unconfirmed reports suggest that the cult attempted to produce and disseminate both botulinum toxin and anthrax before they launched the sarin attack.

"They [the cult] had experts and unlimited funds and laboratories, yet they failed," says Raymond Zilinskas of the University of Maryland Biotechnology Institute. This, he says, is indicative of a significant problem for terrorists: how to transmit the agent and hit the target.

Closer to home, in Antelope, Ore., in 1986, followers of Indian guru Bhagwan Shree Rajneesh contaminated salad bars with salmonella—infecting 750 people—in an effort to influence a local election.

Biological weapons in one form or another can be traced back to 600 B.C. when drinking waters were infected by warring factions. During the 1300s, Tartarians catapulted plague-infested bodies over the city walls of Kaffa—which some say may have initiated the Black Death that raged across Europe. In this century, Japan led a program known as Unit 731 that experimented on humans, including Chinese villagers, with anthrax, cholera, typhoid, plague and typhus. The United States, Canada and the United Kingdom initiated a mini Manhattan Project working to develop offensive biological weapons, but the development of the atomic bomb nullified the project.

"Most of the scenarios talked about deal with the aerosol dissemination of anthrax: a crop duster, put on a spray tank, made in various laboratories," says Simon, who describes anthrax as inexpensive. Botulism also is fairly easy to produce, but the problem is "how to disperse it," says Simon. A disturbing fact is that in the aftermath of the Persian Gulf War it became evident that Iraq had developed agents such as anthrax and botulinum toxin into offensive weapons.

The Iraqis were experimenting with unmanned aircraft equipped with aerosol-spraying devices. If Iraq had perfected this technique it would have been a considerable threat, according to Zilinskas, who served as a member of the UN. Special Commission, or UNSCOM, weapons inspectors investigating Saddam Hussein's arsenals. "Dispersed aerosol anthrax in a terrorist attack is not a big trick. Once they are inoculated with the weapon they are essentially unstoppable."

Iraq admitted to researching offensive uses for anthrax to a UN inspection team in the summer of 1991. Then, in 1995, the country confessed to producing and deploying—prior to the gulf war—aerial bombs, 122-mm rockets, aircraft spray tanks and SCUD missile warheads containing botulinum toxis aflatoxin and anthrax spores, according to the Memorandum to the Biological Weapons Convention Fourth Review Conference, from November 1996.

The U.S. Army predicted use of these weapons would have caused "enormous fatalities" overtaxing the Army's medical-treatment system, according to the August 1997 *Journal of the American Medical Association*, or *JAMA*.

A Department of Defense, or DoD, report identifies nine countries as potential threats in the germ-warfare theater: North Korea, China, India, Pakistan, Iran, Iraq, Libya, Syria and Russia. At the end of last year, the DoD lobbed a preventive strike against biological threats when it announced its decision to inoculate 2.4 million US. soldiers, both active-duty personnel as well as reservists, against anthrax. The $130 million cost will pay for and distribute the vaccine—manufactured by Michigan Biological Products Institute and approved by the Food and Drug Administration—and implement the program during several years.

DoD says it is inoculating against four strains of anthrax and Zilinskas says it would be difficult for any enemy to produce another strain. "When screwing with the organism you might affect its virility or weaken it, making it more susceptible to antibiotic treatment," he says.

In early summer, DoD will begin administering the series of six shots, received by soldiers during an 18-month period, that will counteract the deadly agent that tops the list of biological-warfare threats. Most of the other agents—brucellosis, Q fever, tularemia, smallpox, viral encephalitis, viral hemorrhagic fevers, botulinum and ataphylococcal enterotoxin B (other than the plague)—are much more complicated and require experts to prepare and deliver.

Civilians, who usually are the targets of terrorist attacks, will remain at risk. Simon questions whether it is feasible to vaccinate the entire civilian population but thinks inoculating the military is a "step in the right direction" because they are the first responders to an attack. People infected by anthrax reportedly have survived after early and aggressive treatment, according to *JAMA*.

Zilinskas says UNSCOM is not sure whether Saddam has destroyed the weapons he acquired during the gulf war but thinks the Iraqi dictator's payload has been deactivated since April 1991. Either way the point is moot, muses Zilinskas, because the shelf life of most organisms is only six months. "But they [Iraq] have the people they need, so it would be wise to estimate that they have seed cultures of the organisms they used, so they could probably gear up the biological weapons program in about six months and possibly shorter for limited terrorist use," he adds, noting there still are logistical problems about how to transfer the germs to the terrorists and how to deliver the weapons to the target areas.

The taboo against using such weapons has been broken by state actors as well as by terrorists.

The taboo against using such weapons has been broken by state actors as well as by terrorists. Saddam's use of a witches' brew of gases killing 4,000 Kurds in March 1988 was first, followed by the Japanese doomsday cult's use of sarin nerve gas in the Tokyo subway system. "If you look at public reaction to the World Trade Center and Oklahoma City [bombings], you can multiply it by 10,000 to see the fear and anxiety" that a biological attack would create. "We should improve the readiness of the first responders so they do not fall victim to a first attack," Simon warns. Meanwhile, others advocate increased intelligence work and collaboration between allied intelligent agencies as a defense against this emerging threat.

Harris Arrest Reflects Hatred of City on Racist Right: Germ Warfare in "Jew York"?[3]

For the racist underground, New York is the ultimate Babylon, a seething cauldron of half-human "mud people." Movement zealots, like Larry Wayne Harris, the microbiologist and former Aryan Nations member who watched last week after police seized vials of non-lethal anthrax from him and another man outside of Las Vegas, routinely refer to it as "Jew York."

Harris, author of a self-published book titled *Bacteriological Warfare: A Major Threat to North America*, claims to be simply anxious to find antidotes to germ-warfare agents. However, he not only was a member of the Aryan Nations, but is a follower of Christian Identity, the religious tenet that holds that Jews are the "children of Satan" and minorities are "mud people" who aren't really human.

Harris was on probation after pleading guilty to mail fraud in 1995 when federal authorities charged he falsely stated that a laboratory had authorized him to purchase freeze-dried bubonic plague bacteria, which had been sent to his home. At the time of that arrest, Harris was carrying New York City subway maps, according to a federal law-enforcement official.

William Pierce, head of the National Alliance, author of the *Turner Diaries*, and a former lieutenant to American Nazi leader George Lincoln Rockwell, told the *Charleston* [West Virginia] *Gazette* last week that Harris had approached him in the early 1990s about publishing a book on "how to prepare yourself" for a biological attach. Pierce, whose group has been engaged in an organizing drive in the New York area over the last year, said he declined because he "wasn't convinced of his expertise."

Last summer, Harris spoke to a far-right gathering called the Third Continental Congress in Grandview, Kansas, urging its followers to prepare for biological warfare and obtain antidotes to anthrax. One man who attended the meeting told the *Kansas City Star* last week that following the speech,

---

3. Article by James Ridgeway from the *Village Voice* p.26 Mar. 3, 1998. Copyright © 1998 V. V. Publishng Corporation. Reprinted by permission of the *Village Voice*.

he obtained a quantity of the antibiotic Terramycin from a veterinarian for use as an antidote in the event of an anthrax attack.

For the last few months, the far right has been hyping germ warfare on the Internet and in public meetings. In one recent posting, titled "Anthrax with Love," a correspondent called "Viperfox" urged readers to start taking antibiotics, get immunized with a vaccine, stock up on face masks, and scout out safe refuges by obtaining a survey map from the U.S. Geological Service "listing existing and abandoned mines in your state."

The far right has toyed with the idea of chemical and bacteriological warfare in the past.

The far right has toyed with the idea of chemical and bacteriological warfare in the past. Kerry Noble, a leader of the Covenant, Sword and Arm of the Lord, a militant group active in the 1980s, said the organization was given a container of cyanide by deceased movement leader Bob Miles for possible use in a war against the government. The cyanide was never used.

Dennise Mahon, a former Klan leader and currently Oklahoma leader of White Aryan Resistance, said in an interview last year that in 1991 he received money from the Iraqi embassy in Washington to stage a pro-Iraq rally before the Gulf War.

Klansman-turned-politician David Duke, in his proposal for dividing the country into racial "homelands," suggested that Manhattan and Long Island be declared "West Israel" and that the rest of the metropolitan area become "Minoria," set aside for Puerto Ricans, southern Italians, Greeks, and "other unassimilable minorities."

Arrests Reveal Threat of Biological Weapons[4]

As Federal agents continued to build a case yesterday against two men charged with possessing lethal bacteria, Army scientists proceeded with tests to identify particular strains of disease organisms that might be in confiscated gear.

Culture dishes were being watched closely for features indicating the presence of colonies of Bacillus anthracis, the bacterium that causes anthrax. It can take from 24 to 72 hours for cultures to reveal signs of anthrax, microbiologists said.

Independent scientists who were consulted by the investigative team said samples of DNA from the material recovered in Las Vegas, Nev., were to be sent to the Los Alamos National Laboratory to determine—if anthrax is found—whether it is a deadly variety.

The investigation, coupled with several other recent incidents, prompted some Federal investigators and experts in germ warfare to call for renewed vigilance in the fight to deter biological terror.

Though the Federal Bureau of Investigation and Federal health officials implemented new tactics and rules for tracking and controlling lethal microbes in 1996, a person with a modicum of scientific skill can still readily acquire the means to kill many people, said Frank Scafidi, an F.B.I. spokesman.

"With a little bit of knowledge and a little bit of depravity," Mr. Scafidi said, "you have the makings of a horrendous event."

Bacillus anthracis is frequently shipped between medical research laboratories and can be found in soil after an outbreak in livestock.

"People are shocked that these materials are available," Mr. Scafidi said, referring to anthrax, plague, and the many other infectious diseases that can be used as weapons. "But you're talking about a biological agent that's out there in the natural environment."

The F.B.I. hazardous materials response unit that is pursuing the case was created in 1996, Mr. Scafidi said, in the

---

4. Article by Andrew C. Revkin for the *New York Times* A p7 Feb. 21, 1998. Copyright © 1998 the New York Times Company. Reprinted with permission.

wake of incidents that highlighted the need for more vigilance.

The most dramatic incident was the 1995 sarin gas attacks in Japanese subways by members of the Aum Shinrikyo cult. Twelve people were killed and dozens were hurt.

Japanese investigators discovered that cult members had also obtained anthrax bacteria, apparently by digging up soil where livestock had been infected. They apparently tested, but never perfected, a way to disperse the bacteria spores.

In addition, some cult members traveled to Zaire, possibly to try to obtain ebola virus, one of the deadliest known germs, said John F. Sopko, a longtime aide to former Senator Sam Nunn who conducted investigations leading to the Senate hearings.

"Aum Shinrikyo showed everyone what's possible," Mr. Sopko said.

Another important incident, also in 1995, involved one of the men arrested this week, Larry Wayne Harris.

Mr. Harris, who has training in microbiology, ordered Clostridium botulinum—which produces the botulism toxin, one of the most lethal substances known to science—through the mail from a cell culture repository in Maryland. In a plea agreement, he was convicted on some charges but served no time.

That incident spurred changes in law enforcement and prompted the Federal Centers for Disease Control and Prevention to tighten rules for the handling of 40 deadly organisms. The new rules require laboratories studying the deadliest organisms to register with Federal health officials, have an employee who is certified to handle shipments of the organisms, and be open to inspections.

But an unscrupulous scientist or determined terrorist can still get the makings of a biological bomb, said Amy E. Smithson, an expert in chemical and biological weapons at the Henry L. Stimson Center, a Washington group that studies arms issues.

Cultures of deadly organisms have for many years been circulating overseas. The American Type Culture Collection, the respected nonprofit research group that unwittingly sent Mr. Harris his botulism supply in 1995, legally sent anthrax bacteria to Iraq in the 1980's.

Dozens of diseases that are not lethal enough to make the new Federal list of highly controlled organisms can pose a serious hazard, health officials said.

In Oregon in 1984, followers of Bhagwan Shree Rajneesh seeded salad bars in The Dalles with Salmonella bacteria, sickening 571 of the 10,500 inhabitants.

Even if the substance found in Nevada proves to be anthrax, that does not mean that it was ready to be deployed as a weapon, experts in biological warfare said. The spores can only readily infect people if they are sprayed in an extremely fine mist that can penetrate deep in the lungs, said Dr. Matthew S. Meselson, a biologist at Harvard University.

Still, it is likely only a matter of time before someone uses anthrax or a similar deadly agent, Mr. Sopko said, adding, "It's a realistic threat, both abroad and domestically."

Terrorism, Technology, and the Socioeconomics of Death[5]

The use of biological weapons as a terror weapon should be seen as an inevitability.

Warfare, as an organized endeavor, is facing a paradigmatic shift. Throughout most of history, only states could effectively muster the capacity to kill an enemy in significant numbers. The weakness of the nation-state and the increasing permeability of borders are reducing the effectiveness of the state and increasing the role of non-state actors. Concurrently, the increasingly cheap availability of technical information and dual-use material is making mass killing possible for small groups, or even for individuals. Biological weapons, with their easy accessibility, lack of effective international controls, and disproportionately large effectiveness, offer a singularly attractive mix to radical groups. Due to these changing circumstances, the use of biological weapons as a terror weapon should be seen as an inevitability. The United States must radically rethink how it hopes to deal with biological warfare initiated by terrorists and fringe groups, given the likely ineffectiveness of current policies.

The Present Danger

Humans are creatures of habit. Furthermore, even when confronted with reasonably documented new facts that they understand intellectually, they frequently fail to grasp the new message at the visceral level. The opportunities for mass destruction and "Armageddon on the cheap" have proliferated. Communication and new means of transportation essentially have wiped out the comforts of international isolation. Geography still matters, but it no longer provides a safe haven for any state.

The computer and communications revolution by any measure we wish to cook up, has been taking place at a growth rate of somewhere between 15% and 30% compound for at least the past 30 years. The biotechnology revolution is just beginning and probably will show an even faster growth rate. The implications of these developments, both for the flourishing of civilization and its destruction by means unheard of as early as 30 years ago, are nothing short of staggering.

5. Article by Martin Shubik. First published in *Comparative Strategy* #16 399-414, 1997. Copyright © 1997 Martin Shubik. Reprinted with permission.

Many of the features characteristic of the nation-state of the late nineteenth and early twentieth centuries are becoming obsolete. In particular, borders are highly permeable to individuals, weapons and communication. Changes in technology are intimately intertwined with fundamental changes in the organization and attitudes of society. Transnational firms, associations, and trade patterns are crossing national boundaries with increasing frequency. The intense nationalism and isolationism of pre-World War II is giving way to countries with many small special interest groups, a number of which are well organized with close international connections and may share values far different from the country as a whole. The potential lethality of small, organized, reasonably well-financed groups, be they inside or outside of the country, has been changing by orders of magnitude in the past few decades. The clearly defined concept of deterrence by a large power, if not completely dead, is dying fast for several reasons. There is no longer even an approximately politically bipolar world. Furthermore, the size of the group needed to become an organized agency of mass destruction is fast shrinking to a handful of individuals, less in number than most terrorist organizations.

The amazing feature of today's world is not how bad matters appear to be, but how good they are. With the vast changes that have taken place, the puzzle is why there have not been a far larger series of terrorist-created disasters. The *Economist* (February 3, 1996) presented a graph indicating annual deaths from international terrorism in the past 20 years as fluctuating between 200 and 800 which, in contrast with a Bosnia or Rwanda, is minuscule. Is there some deep implicit set of inhibitions in the human species which keeps it from annihilating itself, or has it just been another instance of plain luck, where the dice have continued to produce apparently improbable rolls?

Open Discussion and Taboos

Prior to writing an article such as this, which deals with some extremely unpleasant topics, several basic and hard to answer questions must be considered. The first is, do we perceive the presence of a qualitatively new danger to our society? The answer clearly is yes. The second question is, is it more or less helpful to write openly about this topic and risk the possibility that it actually might receive public attention of a perverse nature which could hasten the occurrence of the very events we are trying to avoid?

I believe that it is desirable to increase the level of open debate. Given the permeability of communications systems and the nature of modern television and other news media, which treat events such as the Persian Gulf War as though they were baseball playoff games designed more for the convenience of spectators than as a part of history, sooner or later this topic is going to become "popular." My concern is that it should first become popular with the defense establishment and the political community, and that we should start to invest time and resources in doing something about it. Already the World Wide Web is a substantial source for information (or misinformation) on terrorism.

Already the World Wide Web is a substantial source for information (or misinformation) on terrorism.

We must be prepared for the "how-to" articles in *Soldier of Fortune* or even the magazines at the supermarket checkout counters. The Office of Technology Assessment already has provided the curious with a reasonably complete handbook on weapons of mass destruction, with a technical chapter on biological weapons.

Economics, War, and Technology

Economics has been called the dismal science. Military economics may be regarded as the doubly dismal science. It probably is regarded by some as bad taste to investigate the cost of killing and I do not propose to do so in any great detail here. Not only are the data hard to come by, but the clear conceptualization of costs is difficult to formulate well and the relative price level comparisons over the ages are notoriously tricky to construct. Given the level of peasant incomes through the ages, it is my guess is that it probably was rather expensive to kill someone in military action in early history. The deaths per Punt, Shokal, or Drachma probably were depressingly expensive during the growth of civilization. Fortunately for the military planners during early history, communications, transportation, and medicine were sufficiently bad that famine, disease, and death from wounds made the cost-effectiveness figures look somewhat better. But, this is an extremely microeconomics point of view. A more macroeconomics accounting would note that, if virtually all of the peasant population of an occupied territory dies of famine, there may not be enough able-bodied individuals left to plant next year's crops. Indirectly, killing a needed labor force does not add to the cost-effectiveness of one's army. Early in history, the great Chinese general, father of the study of strategy, Sun Tzu, remarked on the dangers of overimpoverishing the peasantry in war.

Yet another problem in calculating the cost of killing comes about in evaluating the costs of being killed and by whom. There do not appear to be any decent publicly available figures of "killed by friendly fire" casualties, but a little consideration of night actions, bombing, and artillery errors, bad visibility, hard to interpret signals, and other aspects of the fog of battle suggest that anywhere from 10% to 20% of one's own forces may not be too bad an estimate for twentieth century war. There is no information on fratricide for Roman, Greek, or other early times that I have been able to locate. The valuation of the loss of one's own human capital stock by self-inflicted killing also should be taken into account when calculating killing costs.

My guess is that the historical peak in killing cost-effectiveness may have been achieved by Genghis Khan and his immediate successors. Their technology did not seem to be much more than good logistics and communications, disciplined cavalry, and the reflex bow. Their decisions to massacre or spare the inhabitants of a captured city appear to have depended considerably on military economic considerations of how expensive it was going to be to capture versus accept a surrender, and what the administrative cost and threat to logistics a potential revolt would entail. In the writings on Genghis Khan, there appears to be some evidence that the Mongols tended to spare the lives of the better artisans.

The estimated deaths from the Mongol invasion of China appear to be staggering, but preponderately due to famine and plague rather than straightforward military killing. I doubt the accuracy of both the figures for overall world population and the count of Mongol inflicted casualties, but a guesstimate of between 8% and 12% of world population probably is not too far from the mark, counting slaughter, disease, and famine. In modern terms, on a percentage basis, this is as though the United States and the former Soviet Union had succeeded in wiping out each other in a nuclear war.

Cost-and-Demand Elasticities of Weapons Systems, Externalities, and the Game

Any good defense economist can point out one of the paradoxes of new weaponry. Not only may the cost of a weapons system far outstrip the initial estimates; every new system for offense generates a new system for defense, and thus the supply generates a new direct demand.

The strategic aspects of the economics of weapons development call for a continuous flow of improvement and innovation. Costs and supplies are in a constant state of flux. Many externalities are generated in the course of production, and these externalities easily may be of considerable negative or positive worth to society as a whole. A specific example is provided by the more or less unforeseen costs of disposal of nuclear waste. On the positive side, much of the revolution in air transportation and in communications after World War II can be attributed to the military developments during that war.

One of the perceived values of the atomic bomb was going to be "more bang for the buck" and the societal spin-off was going to be "virtually free electrical energy." The early cost estimates did not match the current realities.

The basic lethal components are cheap and can be manufactured in small batches with relative ease.

Innovation is critical to weapons development. But, the economics of innovation dictates that new product development and testing tend to be expensive. Once this stage has been passed, costs depend heavily on innovation in the methods of production and on being able to use mass production techniques. While this has been shown to be highly relevant in the development of nuclear weapons, aircraft, tanks, artillery, and communications systems, the direction in biological warfare appears to be different. The basic lethal components are cheap and can be manufactured in small batches with relative ease.

The Communication Revolution and the Weakening of the Nation-State

The telegram and telephone are not much more than a century old. Radio is younger, television is a little older than a half century, the high-speed digital computer is slightly younger, and the personal computer and mass market cellular phone are younger still.

In the 1950s, much of the thinking about the role of the computer was biased toward its role as a great centralizing and controlling device. In the early 1960s, time-sharing firms envisioned great central computer installations much like central powerhouses. The invention of the personal computer completely changed the nature of usage. Today, the power of a personal computer, combined with new printing devices, the fax machine, and computer networks, has been an enormous force for decentralization. Any small organized group can economically print and distribute its message. Small common interest groups can be in touch by e-mail, the world over. The monopoly, or even partial monopoly, of a central government or large corporation over the means of communication had been shattered. National boundaries pose, at best, weak barriers to communication. At considerable expense, with vigilance, it still is possible to patrol national borders to prevent citizens from leaving or to catch illegal immigrants. A certain amount of control can be exercised over the flow of goods, but illegal immigration and the drug trade both attest to the growing permeability of world borders.

Even 30 or 40 years ago a well-organized dictatorship could suppress the physical means for information dissemination. This is becoming less and less feasible. The availability of new communications devices defeats the capabilities of even a dedicated police state.

Unfortunately, as it is with most changes, a shift which apparently cures one problem can easily create another. In particular, the speed with which misinformation, distortions, biased selections from the whole picture, and pure lies can be disseminated greatly exacerbates the instability of mob behavior and creates the potential for mistaken premature action based on the passions of the moments as magnified by the mass media.

Tied in with the growth of communications networks in general, science and finance in particular, has come the opportunity for attacks on mass communications systems by small groups or individuals. The recent publication by T. Shimomura, with J. Markoff illustrated the amount of damage that can be done by a single malicious "hacker" and the vulnerability of communications systems to sophisticated sabotage.

The End of Deterrence: Identification, Friend or Foe (IFF) and the Cable News Network (CNN)

The period from 1945 until the breakup of the Soviet Union, more or less, was a time of a bipolar world. The war game contained the Red and the Blue. SIOP was aimed against RISOP (the United States and Soviet Union strategic nuclear plans). Damage exchange models could be worked out in fair detail with plenty of technical input and, depending on the level of aggregation and classification, even an amateur war gamer could paper his game room or study with a map of the United States and the Soviet Union with anywhere between a few dozen to many hundreds of targets with different priorities.

The heritage of Herman Kahn, Tom Schelling, Albert Wohlstetter, and several others built up a rich literature of ploy and counterploy; threat and counterthreat. A verbal, dynamic, two-person, nonzero sum, game theory debate flourished between individuals concerned with the plausibility of the threats employed and the defenses offered. Jesuitical (or Talmudic) fine points appeared in deciding when an act touted as defensive really was defensive or should be interpreted as offensive. But, all the way through this golden age of deterrence in a bipolar world, there were several implicit assumptions which are fast becoming obsolete.

The disparity in size among the five atomic powers (and the one or two more suspected atomic powers) was so great that, for many purposes, a good approximation of the "game" was between two coalitions.

Leaving aside the relative sizes of the powers, all of the analysis was based on the nation-state as the irreducible unit of action. The Irish Republican Army (IRA), the Red Brigades, the Hezbollah, Hamas were regarded as irrelevant to the conversation. The "crazies" could be an annoyance. They could place a car bomb here or blow up an embassy there. But, the casualties generated were to be measured at most in the tens and, by some stretch of the imagination, if the World Trade Center had not been so badly botched, maybe a few hundred or a thousand or two. Our conventional thought reserves the delivery of quick "megadeaths" as the domain of the major nation-state. But, with the change in technology, a well-organized, reasonably well-financed group of even less than a few dozen may be able to acquire a lethality larger than an atomic bomb.

In one of the Gilbert and Sullivan light operas, it is observed that "things are seldom what they seem." In the world of CNN, a good riot staged so that it takes place at prime time might even be worth financing.

The coverage of the Persian Gulf War from Baghdad was not too far from having an American Jewish reporter interview Adolph Hitler at Treblinka. It is getting harder and harder to know who the actors are and what they are doing in a world of instant feedback. This is especially true where the entertainment value of war has increased and, instead of Madame La Farge having to go to a crowded square to see the guillotine, where at most only a few hundred could have ringside seats, we now have the opportunity to create mood swings in millions at the same time. If country A has unfriendly relations with country B, and there is a small country C, or a small group within that country, which hates them both—if mass destruction were cheap enough, a major incident could be created by the third party in country A covered on prime time giving broad visibility to false clues provided by the perpetrators attributing the act to the perfidy of country B. The combination of virtually on-line communications with little improvement in IFF adds a new dimension to the world ahead.

A key element in much of old deterrence theory was that the nation and its potential foes were reasonably well informed about each other and that the IFF problem was kept to a minimum. Even then, there still would be some "Launch on Warning" problems to be considered to avoid the inadvertent start of World War III. But, on the whole, everyone had a program, knew who the actors were, and had a reasonably good view of their behavioral patterns. It is much more difficult to deter when you do not know who you are deterring. In spite of the Serbs, Croats, and Bosnians or the Hutu and the Tutsi, large groups of individuals, at least up to a point, appear to have some desire for survival. When one reads history in general and the history of religion in particular, it is not too difficult to locate small groups, both here and abroad, as their lethality increases.

The shift away from a bipolar world, together with the permeability of borders and the lethality of small groups, means that the burden of defense has increased. This increase has occurred because the old defense commitments have not gone away; they merely have been modified and new commitments have been added. We must be better prepared to fight many different types of war, ranging from global nuclear, conventional small wars, police actions, and now highly lethal terrorist activities which can arise from the actions of solitary psychotics, fringe ideological groups, criminal, or third-party sponsored agents.

The Biologist's War

It has been suggested by Alan Beyerchen that World War I was the chemist's war. The fixation of nitrogen, the improvement in the nature and manufacturing of explosives, and the manufacturing of poison gas changed the technology of war. World War II was the physicist's (and engineer's) war with the advent of the atomic bomb, radar, and rocket systems. The cold war saw the proliferation of computation and communications. Integrated defense networks of a size and complexity unheard of a few years earlier became a viable possibility. The future, however, Beyerchen has suggested, may belong to the biologist. World War III easily could be the biologist's war.

World War III easily could be the biologist's war.

Although it never made front-page news until recently, when the United States and Russia indicated that they wished to cease the stockpiling of materials for chemical or biological warfare, a substantial subindustry existed both in the United States and elsewhere from the 1950s onward, until Nixon terminated the program in 1971. It fortunately is difficult to obtain trustworthy open literature estimates on expenditures on chemical and biological warfare. Even if we had them, a considerable conceptual cleanup would be needed to make sure that the categories meaningfully reflected the purpose. A crude guesstimate is that the United States may have spent somewhere between $50 billion and $150 billion on such a program.

An interesting exercise for those concerned with the accuracy of information would be to study the Central Intelligence Agency (CIA) and other U.S. estimates of Soviet military expenditures and compare them with the information that we now have obtained from Russia. The observations above on numbers can be translated operationally as "a moderately large amount of money was spent" on chemical and biological warfare prior to the formal discontinuation of the program.

With the breakup of the Soviet Union (or the Russian empire, as some may view it) a certain amount of information concerning their work in biological warfare has come through to the West. The new horsemen of the Apocalypse in scholarly, scientific, and military garb, both in Russia and the United States, have smallpox, anthrax, plague, botulism, and many more items on the list to add to crop dusting, air conditioning systems, water supplies, food, and other means of mass distribution.

Unlike the development of nuclear technology and modern physics, all the economic indicators point to the goal of "killing on the cheap" actually being realized.

The Revolution in Biotechnology: Innovation and Costs

Possibly the most exciting part of modern science at this time is biology. In the past 50 years, there has been an explosion in knowledge which at least equals and possibly dwarfs the computer revolution. Furthermore, the pace probably is increasing. The pace of development, by almost any growth measure, appears to be anywhere from 20% to 40% per annum. The production of new chemical compounds and biological agents is being revolutionized. New substances— some of which may be lethal, others beneficial—can be created at a rate undreamed of previously. As noted by M. Dando, "What would require the skills of a Nobel Prize winner in one decade will become common laboratory practice in the next. All or almost all countries have the ability to produce deadly biotoxins cheaply."

From the economist's point of view, what is happening in biological technology is not unlike what has happened in computer technology. In the beginning, there were IBM, UNIVAC, and a few others. The forecasters (including myself) were dead wrong. The industry did not remain one where entry would be virtually impossible due to the need for. enormous capital investment. The trend toward centralization and the public utility image was reversed. Not only was the quasi-monopoly of IBM destroyed, so was the quasi-monopoly of AT&T. Today, whether it is computations or communications or in hardware or software (a distinction which is becoming more and more fuzzy), a few individuals with relatively modest financing have a sporting chance to go into business for themselves. The odds are that biotechnology is heading in the same direction. Not only do the costs of producing deadly substances appear to be plunging, but the size of the minimum viable manufacturing unit is small and the capital investment is being reduced. Furthermore, unlike the old-fashioned nuclear devices and their delivery systems, the means of delivery (although still an important and dangerous bottleneck) do not appear to be particularly expensive or require large centralized capital investment.

In the language of the old-time economist, the long-run costs appear to be falling and the industry probably will become more competitive with the barriers to entry low and the possibilities for small producers in specialized niches reasonably good.

The Lethality of a Small Group

It has been suggested that history is a description of what happened by the winners or the descendants of the winners. Most winners tend not to boast about the massacres and disasters that they caused. If required to explain some unfortunate incident, humans have an ability to rationalize that far exceeds any ability in rational thought. Thus, a successful religion concentrates on shrines and festivals for its martyrs. Somehow, if a hundred or a thousand savages or unbelievers were slaughtered for every martyr celebrated, these individuals would be forgotten or their deaths regarded as incidental to a just cause.

Killing and the techniques for killing are not pleasant topics. Contemplating the cost and convenience of killing through the ages might even be regarded as bad taste by some. But, unfortunately, it is necessary.

In the attempt to blow up the World Trade Center, an extra bar or two of spent plutonium would have made south Manhattan uninhabitable for a considerable time. Given the level of security at nuclear generating plants, the possibility for successful theft exists, but safe transportation certainly would cause an unskilled group some problems.

The history of development of the technology of warfare is a fascinating topic in and of itself. A brief and highly incomplete weapons list over time includes club, knife, sword, spear, shield, trident, trireme, reflex bow, cavalry, saddle, stirrup, crossbow, long-bow, gunpowder, barque, siege gun, rifle, revolver, telegraph, telephone, railway, dreadnought, long-range artillery, machine gun, poison gas, submachine gun, plane, bomb, tank, helicopter, bazooka, submarine, computer, atomic bomb, modern artillery, rocket delivery system, and now biological warfare.

The advent of each item in its time involved not merely technology, but financing, the economics of manufacturing, and shifts in logistics and organization. The shifts, as units such as the battleship grew larger, called for more centralized organization and formalized routine for running many hundreds of individuals, who were strangers, in the same ship. Better logistics enabled army size to grow and called for the creation of a general staff to aid the commanding general. But, not all innovations call for bigger size and more organization. An increase in lethality or mobility of a small unit, be it a ship, tank, or commando group, can send the size requirements down, not up.

. . . The social sciences are notorious for drawing graphs and diagrams with ill-defined measures on the axes and showing items which are poorly quantified. I suggest that it may be worth attempting to sketch such a diagram, provided that the conceptual difficulties in measurement are explained and the diagram is interpreted merely as a device to sweeten the intuition or promote debate.

The horizontal axis indicates historical time. The vertical axis requires much specification and the leeway for alternative constructions is great. In essence, the question to be answered is, what casualties can be inflicted by a small organized group of, say, 10 to 20 trained, dedicated individuals in a single action? The word "casualty" is vague. Do we mean killed during the action: dead from wounds several days, months, or years later (as with radiation); or dead from starvation or disease indirectly caused by the action? How do we classify events, such as the burning of Rome or London, which could have been random or could have been arson? This sort of killing requires a probability measure. The conventional casualty counts, even for nuclear warfare, require lower and upper bounds and some form of expected value. In spite of the elaborate computations, complete with maps and diagrams around ground zero, the numbers presented can vary by an order of magnitude with a wind change or heavy rain at an appropriate time.

Raids by small groups of brigands or outlaws do not appear to last for more than a few hours. Strikes by terrorists tend to be even shorter. Although the load-reload time of the long-bow might be regarded as the harbinger of the trend toward automatic or multiple-shot long-distance weapons, it is difficult to conceive of a longbowman killing more than an average of one per 5 minutes for a 3- or 4-hour day. Close quarters weaponry, such as the sword, would have an even lower yield.

Mass executions, such as the crucifixions after the Spartacus rebellion, or the guillotine in the French terror, or mass murders in the German death camps, appear to be somewhat labor intensive and to require considerable organization. Hence, even if only a few actual direct killers are involved, they require at least the legal and usually the logistic support of the society or an occupying power. Terrorist or other dissident groups do not have this luxury. They may have financing, and some logistics, and communications provided by an outside power. But, in general, they do not have immediate local social and legal acceptance.

I suggest that, from 5000 B.C. to possibly as late as 1950 A.D., a comfortable upper bound on the lethality of a dissident group in any action was of the order of 1,000, where the count was limited to killed directly or died from wounds. Since 1950, the change in the technology of killing devices and in logistics and communications, has been exponential. I have not yet been able to find clear examples of a dissident or terrorist strike exceeding a thousand fatal casualties (although the Aum Shinrikyo incident in March 1995 when a near miss with 10 dead and several thousand injured), but without having to overdo the James Bond scenarios, the technology, logistics, and communications have been in place for at least the past 20 years and, since then and into the immediate future, the lethality is increasing to the point that by year 2000 the ability of such a group to wipe out a major city of 5 million to 10 million is highly probable.

By year 2000 the ability of such a group to wipe out a major city of 5 million to 10 million is highly probable.

A statistic that possibly is even more relevant, and even harder to come by, is the lethality of a single individual or a group of two or three. One of the pleasant paradoxes of human affairs is that secrets are best kept by one individual. A group of two can be reasonably silent. Possibly, three can keep an extremely low profile. But, above three, the chances for leaks due to boasting, sloppiness, interception of messages, or other causes increase considerably. Unfortunately, the lethality of the pathological behavior of the lone gunman has increased considerably by the availability of automatic weapons. The probability of detecting some individual in a group of size above one, as the group grows, soon becomes substantial in comparison to the probability of detecting a single pathological individual before it is too late.

The Dog That Did Not Bark

I return to my opening Panglossian theme. Why are matters as good as they are? Why was the World Trade Center job botched so badly and carried out with so little imagination? Why did the Aum Shinrikyo fail to bring off mass murder? Has there been a vast underground growth, during which the system gathers energy underground, not unlike a mushroom prior to emerging aboveground? A sign of underground activity is provided by reports of the discovery of accidents. Every now and then a Weatherman managed to blow up itself with a badly built bomb. The safety of nuclear plants was brought into question by the disaster at Cherno-byl. The anthrax accident at Sverdlovsk (April 1979) was a harbinger of the brave new world. But, the information originally was distorted, and the magnitude and implication of the casualties came out in drips and drabs. Possibly, somewhere in the Pentagon or in the archives of the CIA are estimates of the number of accidents which already have taken place in the United States at Richmond or Los Alamos, or in Iraq or France or elsewhere, involving contagion and death while testing a nuclear device or a man-made disease transmission device.

In August 1994, several individuals were arrested at the Munich Airport, purportedly as couriers for the transportation of weapons grade plutonium. It was conjectured that Russian scientists probably were selling it to customers such as the Libyans and Iranians in order to replace the salaries that they no longer were receiving. The sale of Siberian experimental nuclear reactors to the Chinese was another way of supplementing income. Are we just crying "wolf," or are we victims of too much science fiction? I suspect that the danger is real.

Is it that we are confronted with deep biological, sociological, or psychological inhibitors? What are the inhibitions? If they exist, do we expect them to last? I suspect that they exist at all levels and we appear to know little about them. However, even with little knowledge, it is a safe bet that, as the weaponry becomes cheaper and requires fewer individuals for delivery, a threshold will be reached where there will be enough socially alienated, mad, or fanatical individuals to break taboos or overcome the inhibitions.

A threshold will be reached where there will be enough socially alienated, mad, or fanatical individuals to break taboos or overcome the inhibitions [of using the weaponry].

Precedent and Inhibitions

Our legal system pays much attention to precedent. There are actions which "civilized societies" do not take. Thus, to many of us, the death chambers of Nazi Germany or the rape of Nanking verge on the incomprehensible. Yet, when we go down the checklist on the use of chemical, biological, and nuclear warfare, this century, there are precedents for all three. The gas attacks in World War I, the atomic bombing of Japan, and the activities of Japan's Unit 731 provided the evidence. The poisoning of wells offers earlier historical precedent. It is evident that the unthinkable already has been thought and has served as a basis for action. W. Laqueur suggested that there have been amateurish attempts in the

United States and abroad utilizing botulism, ricin (twice), sarin (twice), bubonic plague bacteria, typhoid bacteria, hydrogen cyanide, and VX nerve gas.

A Note on Capital Stock

The world has made great strides toward economic liberalization. There clearly has been a decrease in Communist dictatorships and a growth of more or less free enterprise democracies. The threat of nuclear warfare carried with it twin levels of destruction. It wipes out both human beings and capital stock. The switch to biological warfare (to use a little ecotalk) is that it can be used primarily to destroy "human capital" leaving the physical capital stock intact. Thus, the survivors in a world with reduced population could be potentially richer, not poorer, on a per capita basis than the nuclear war survivors, if they can prevent the capital stock from deteriorating.

This last remark is made partly facetiously, but there is a deep anthropological problem which cannot be dismissed merely because it appears to be in bad taste. Is there a sociobiological aspect to war? Could this be the way that our species, with its limited intelligence, keeps an upper bound on its population? Prior to World War II, the anthropology of war received some attention.

In some instances "it is hard to tell the good guys from the bad guys without a program." Legitimacy is often a subject for debate, and the debate may be violent. When viewed through the eyes of previous occupants of positions of power or viewed many years after the fact, the use of force by Oliver Cromwell, George Washington, Simón Bolivar, Napoleon Bonaparte, Sun Yat-sen, Vladimir Lenin, Joseph Stalin, Adolph Hitler, Fidel Castro, Saddam Hussein, or Hafiz Assad raises some uncomfortable questions. When is a liberation movement dangerous and wicked, and when is it part of the progress toward a democratic society? The Irgun, the Muslim Brotherhood, Hamas, the IRA, the Tamil Tigers, and the fighters for the Basque homeland or a Puerto Rico independence group all have some basis for legitimacy in someone's eyes.

Beyond the nationalists are those with social and religious causes. Thus, we have the Baader Meinhoff, the Branch Davidians, the Aum Shinrikyo, the Hezbollah, and various apocalyptic movements and freedom militia.

There possibly are five groupings worth considering separately:
1.   national liberators;
2.   social and religious causes;
3.   criminal groups;
4.   "rational" malcontents and disaffected; and
5.   the nonsocial, psychotic, and otherwise alienated socially pathological

One might expect biological attack blackmail from groups 3 or 4, but can expect usage from the three other groups.

Table 1: Economics and Technology

	Nuclear	Biological	Chemical
Procurement	Hard	Relatively easy	Relatively easy
Manufacture	Hard	Relatively easy	Relatively easy
Storage	Difficult	Difficult	Difficult
Delivery	Hard	Hard and hazardous	Hard and hazardous
Group size	Fair-sided group	Few	Few
Lethality	High	High	High
Target control	Fair	Poor	Poor
Property damage	High	Low	Low
Cost effectiveness	So-so to good	Very good	Very good
Detection	High	Low	Low

Table I provides some quick current technological and economic comparisons of nuclear, biological, and chemical weaponry.

The Economic Future for Chemical and Biological War

There still appear to be technical problems in the military use, and clean delivery and control, of chemical and biological weapons; in my estimation the more immediate danger lies elsewhere. All but one of the technical problems calling for innovation have legitimate, peaceful, productive reasons for solution: They are better transportation, packaging, and materials handling of deadly substances. The one purely hostile problem is weapons delivery, and it is in the self-interest of a small country to solve the delivery problem. It is likely that all of these will be solved in a relatively inexpensive manner. When they are, the potential for cheap, clandestine manufacture and delivery of chemical and biological weapons will show the characteristics of the Ameriean economic dream. It will become a growth industry, with ease of entry; more and more room for small individual entrepreneurs with capital requirements no more complex than a minibrewery; many "promising" alternative products, a high level of innovation, and falling costs in procurement, manufacture, and delivery.

A Program for the Future

In a world where the stable door is usually closed after the horse has escaped, how do we disseminate what is known and what can we do about these new possibilities without creating panic and possibly encouraging deviant behavior? It is almost conventional wisdom that the military prepare for the last war. It also is a reasonably accurate view of public political behavior that, after a substantial "peace scare" such as the breakup of the Soviet Union, there is considerable pressure to cut defense spending. In spite of the end of the cold war, now is the time, unfortunately, to increase defense research on the unseen war. There is no easy solution available, but there are a few obvious steps to be taken.

1. Possibly the highest priority item is the least technical and least obvious. The responsibilities of the armed forces, police forces, Federal Bureau of Investigation (FBI), CIA, and the security agencies must be redefined in order to prevent "turf wars," bureaucratic foulups, jurisdictional fights, and bureaucratic confusion in major emergencies. The clarification of responsibility and coordination of action in the event of high lethality terrorist activity is vital. Casualties in the thousands are not matters merely for the police and FBI. It not only is a matter of recarving up jurisdictions, but a way for decisive coordinated action must be available. The jurisdictional problems are considerable, even in trying to capture a solitary computer hacker-saboteur as illustrated in the pursuit of Kevin Mitnick. The distinctions among conventional war, nonconventional war, and terrorism are being

blurred by the changes in magnitudes. The missions of the conventional armed forces, police forces, and surveillance agencies must be reconsidered.

2. The legal aspects of search and detainment must be reconsidered in view of the trade-off between individual rights and the magnitude of casualties feasible without prompt action. The compiling of potential terrorist lists and the surveillance of suspected individuals and organizations pose many sticky problems concerning civil liberty and the public right to know. Will we need a major disaster in order to revamp our procedures?

3. The dual-purpose aspects of the biotechnology production facilities and the ease of production pose considerable difficulties in the construction of a monitoring system that is not unduly bureaucratic and cumbersome. The problem of surveillance is well known and already has been addressed. It must be designed with the full understanding that a tight policing, such as is possible for nuclear fuel, is not feasible.

The three items noted above require attention and action now. There also are several open questions which require basic scholarly research.

4. A multidisciplinary program is required for the study of the psychiatric and socio-psychological profiles of terrorists and the alienated. There probably is an important distinction to be made between the pathological loner, criminals, and those with "a cause." An international comparison would be highly desirable.

5. We need to understand the positive and negative aspects of public education to major terrorist threat. Does the providing of information produce an "imitation effect"? Will showing individuals how to wipe out a town on the cheap produce an imitation effect as soon as one incident has taken place? How hard is the evidence that publicity concerning one event of bottle tampering triggers more events of bottle tampering? There may be no clean answers that hold for all populations. This is much like the question facing an air force general. Should he or she inform his or her pilots of the statistics on their probability of being killed on a bombing mission? The answer probably depends on the personality of the pilot.

6. A somewhat scholarly, and not immediately applicable, question concerns man in particular and primates in general. Are there inhibiting forces which mitigate against a species self-destructing? Has the gap between technology and aver-

age intelligence and social organization reached a crisis level which makes self-destruction a serious possibility?

7. What are the symptoms of the new danger and how do we design systems to cope with them? What are the new false signals going to look like? There is good evidence that a considerable percentage of the airline bomb scares were calls put in by individuals who would miss their plane unless they could delay it for an hour or two. How large and reactive must a bioterrorism counterforce be? How badly overloaded will the system be with false alarms?

8. The legal system must keep up with the problems generated by the increasing manufacture of new toxic substances. This includes laws concerning registration, sale, transport, and possession. Can this system be designed to avoid Big Brother and deadly bureaucracy?

The legal system must keep up with the problems generated by the increasing manufacture of new toxic substances.

9. The doctrine of deterrence in a multipolar, clearly nationalist world still has a role. But, it is no longer enough. The simplistic "we and they" division to describe potential combat also is no longer enough. There not merely is an enemy, but potentially many small enemies from within, some of which may have other national or transnational sponsors. The IFF problems often have been solved on the battlefield by applying the maxim "shoot first, ask questions later." This does not seem to be a totally satisfying solution to what lies ahead. The concept of threat must be revisited. But, the subtleties to be faced go far beyond the disturbing, yet relatively simple, nuclear war world of Herman Kahn.

10. A new offensive weapon brings with it the research on defense and the counterweapons. Massive inoculations against some of the biowar diseases may be technologically feasible, but the economics quickly limits what can be done. The economics of defense does not look promising, but considerable study is needed.

Appendix 1: A Cautionary Primer

The poet Samuel Hoffenstein, in his verse "Cradle Song" wrote:

Fear not the atom in fission:
The cradle will outwit the hearse;
Man on this earth has a mission—
To survive and go on getting worse.

We should hope that his optimism is justified. A look at the activities at Sverdlovsk, Porton Down, Camp Detrick, Pine

Bluff, or Ping Fan is not comforting. In 1972, approximately 120 nations signed the Biological and Toxic Weapons Convention. This was a step in the right direction but, unfortunately, adherence by nation-states is not enough.

Not only is the technology becoming cheap, the chances are growing for dual purpose machinery suited, for example, for both a minibrewery and for less pleasant purposes.

The idea of biological warfare, at least in implicit form, is not new. It is probable that both the Greeks and Romans used infected corpses to poison wells. It has been suggested that Lord Amhurst presented the Indians with smallpox-infected blankets. In more modern times, at Ping Fan, Unit 731 of the Japanese army may have been responsible for several thousand "experimental science" deaths. The Iraqi-Iranian war saw chemical use on the Kurds. The actual deaths to date are minor in comparison with Hiroshima, Nagasaki, or the Dresden, Hamburg, and Tokyo firestorms. But, bean counting or corpse counting are not the appropriate measures. Our concern is with the shape of things to come.

V. Is the U.S. Prepared?

Editor's Introduction

In November 1998, a group of leaders and scientists from around the world met at Stanford University in California to discuss scientific topics relevant to international affairs. They concluded that biological and chemical warfare are currently the two most serious dangers to humanity. Amid all this recent furor raised over chemical and biological weapons, the issue of U.S. preparedness must inevitably be raised. Is the United States capable of dealing with the threat of chemical or biological attack, and if not, what is being done to change that? There has been no proven use of biological or chemical tactics on American soil, but most observers agree that the possibility of a catastrophe definitely exists. The recent proliferation of militia groups within the United States, as well as the suspicions of certain nations such as Iraq and North Korea possessing illegal chemical/biological stockpiles, demonstrate that our nation must be able to protect its citizens. Many argue that during the Cold War, defensive measures against nuclear weapons to a certain extent deterred their use; the importance of taking precautions against chemical and biological weapons is therefore undeniable, regardless of exactly how real history may eventually show the danger to have been.

The articles contained in this final chapter assess the current level of U.S. preparedness and the outlook for the near future. In the first article, "The Threat of Germ Weapons Is Rising. Fear, Too," William J. Broad and Judith Miller examine how chemical and biological warfare has suddenly emerged as a paramount threat in the past few years. The dangers posed by both terrorists and potential enemy nations are also discussed in this *New York Times* piece, and a general summary of preliminary U.S. precautions—such as the vaccination of American troops—is given.

A second *New York Times* article by Broad and Miller, "Exercise Finds U.S. Unable to Handle Germ War Threat," describes exactly what the title suggests. Here the authors report on a secret training exercise in which federal officials simulated a terrorist germ attack in order to test their abilities to handle such a crisis. The discouraging result was total disaster, as the participants were unable to mount a successful, united response. The major positive outcome of the experiment is that it brought further awareness in government of the need to improve.

In the chapter's third and last *New York Times* article, John M. Broder addresses President Clinton's recent proposals for dealing with "unconventional" terrorist attack. In addition to chemical and biological agents, these unconventional methods include the infiltration of computer systems. The president stresses that these new threats need to be taken seriously, and that the arena of military conflict is shifting from "land, sea, and air to the human body" itself. Among Clinton's plans are allocating nearly $3 billion for such purposes as the creation of urban medical emergency teams, developing the necessary medicines to counteract germ agents, and raising the general awareness of the American public as to the threat involved.

An American Forces Press Service article from *National Guard* magazine, "Senate Raps Investigation, Chemical Warfare Training," approaches the issue of U.S. preparedness by looking back on the way the government handled the results of a previous incident of alleged chemical attack, namely the so-called Gulf War syndrome. Many believe that this illness arose due to the exposure of American troops to Iraqi chemical agents during the Persian Gulf conflict. The article reports on a 1998 Senate investigation into the nation's ability to react to chemical and biological attack. This investigation also criticized the way the federal government responded to the complaints of Persian Gulf veterans claiming to be suffering from Gulf War syndrome.

Finally, the last piece included in this chapter comes from *U.S. News & World Report*. "The New Terror Fear: Biological Weapons," by Nicholas Horrock, begins with an assessment of the government's first implementation of the Domestic Preparedness program, in Denver, Colorado. Recent events calling for the need for such preparedness are summed up by the author, most notably the looming threat of Iraq. The logistics of detecting and identifying a biological attack is also discussed at length, including descriptions of current technology. The article closes with a description of a 1997 anthrax scare in Washington, D.C.

The Threat of Germ Weapons Is Rising. Fear, Too[1]

U.S. troops in the Persian Gulf are vaccinated against deadly germs. So are FBI agents who are probing a growing number of biological incidents. So are some White House officials.

Protections against living weapons are new to the military and security of the United States, and they raise troubling questions.

Is this prudence or paranoia? Should everyone be vaccinated? How real is the threat? Aren't deadly germs nearly impossible for attackers to use without hurting themselves? Isn't this threat just another bogeyman, like so many before?

Germ weapons, though around for centuries, have played no significant role in modern warfare and terrorism. Skeptics point to this history and say that biological strikes of any consequence are unlikely.

Is this prudence or paranoia? Should everyone be vaccinated? How real is the threat?

But officials in Washington from President Clinton on down are taking the issue very seriously, with thousands of people and billions of dollars in motion to address the germ threat.

"Eventually, this is going to hurt us," said Robert Blitzer, who recently left the FBI after directing its section on domestic terrorism. "There's no question in my mind."

Moreover, a yearlong inquiry by the *New York Times* revealed trends that suggest the era of germ tranquility may indeed be ending:

- Uprooted weapon scientists from Iraq, Russia and South Africa are hunting for new jobs and spreading germ secrets.
- Radical states with reputations for supporting terror, such as Iran and Libya, are seeking germ weapons.
- Terrorists, including Osama bin Laden, are increasingly interested in pestilential germs. Some boast openly of being able to kill foes with deadly plagues.

Today, officials in Washington stress that they know of no imminent danger, even while acknowledging the limitations of intelligence. Most agree that the threat, while low, is growing.

The defenses that Washington is quietly erecting, officials say, are akin to the insurance that homeowners take out

---

1. Article by William J. Broad and Judith Miller from the *New York Times* Dec. 27, 1998. Copyright © 1998 the New York Times Company. Reprinted with permission.

against floods and earthquakes. The odds may be small, this argument goes, but precautions are warranted since conditions are changing and damage could be great.

R. James Woolsey, director of Central Intelligence from 1993 to 1995, is among the former officials who are worried. Germ terrorism, he said in an interview, is "the single most dangerous threat to our national security in the foreseeable future."

Germ weapons can be hard to make and use, contrary to myth and claim. It took the United States decades to master the art before renouncing such arms in 1969. In the early 1990s, Aum Shinrikyo, a Japanese cult, launched at least nine germ attacks in Tokyo that were meant to kill millions. But the strikes produced no known injuries or deaths.

Germ weapons can be hard to make and use, contrary to myth and claim. It took the United States decades to master the art before renouncing such arms in 1969.

Dangerous to the attacker as well as the attacked if successful, germ weapons are considered most practical when used far from the aggressor's homeland; intervening land and sea establish what amounts to a quarantine.

The main appeal of such weapons is that they are incredibly cheap compared to chemical and atomic arms. Yet pound for pound, germ weapons rival nuclear ones for maiming and killing, and some biological agents are considered superior in that regard; in theory they can annihilate many millions of people.

Clearly, they surpass their nuclear kin as an instrument of fright and disruption: Once sown, infections can spread unpredictably, since they are alive. Experts especially worry about smallpox, which is highly contagious and seen as particularly dangerous since few people are now immunized against its ravages.

"To say the threat is low is not to minimize its potential," said Neil Gallagher, assistant director for national security at the FBI.

Today, the secrets of germ warfare are increasingly up for grabs as weapon scientists from countries that made biological arsenals hunt for new jobs. The nomads are from Iraq (starting in 1991 after Persian Gulf war), Russia (starting in 1992 after the Soviet collapse) and South Africa (starting in 1994 as apartheid fell apart). Russia alone has many thousands of former germ warriors increasingly cold, poor and hungry.

Legitimate science also heightens the risk. The global war against infectious disease has produced more than 1,500 germ banks that tend to trade freely in deadly microbes.

Future strides could make matters even worse. Experts agree that research into the genetic foundations of life, an approach that promises to cure many diseases, might, in evil hands, one day produce weapons that work against only certain races or ethnic groups.

"It's difficult but not impossible," said Dr. Joshua Lederberg, a Nobel laureate in biology who advises Washington on germ warfare. More unsettling, he added, is that traditional killers seem to be a growing danger right now; he called them "a monster in the back yard."

Today, at least 17 nations are suspected of having or trying to acquire germ weapons. Perhaps they want to deter foes. The wild card is that some (Cuba, Iran, Iraq, Libya, North Korea, Syria) are also considered architects of terrorism.

Today, at least 17 nations are suspected of having or trying to acquire germ weapons.

Libya worked hard to join the germ club. In 1994, it sought to hire scientists fleeing South Africa's crumbling program, including its head, Dr. Wouter Basson. That move, officials say, was foiled by diplomatic pressure from Washington and London.

However, Libya may have succeeded in hiring (or perhaps hiding and employing for Baghdad) Dr. Amir Medidi, a top scientist of Iraq's germ effort, U.N. inspectors revealed.

Terrorists themselves seem increasingly drawn to germ weapons.

Osama bin Laden, the renegade Saudi millionaire known for his bitter hatred of America, is investigating them, U.S. officials say. Whether his work has resulted in secret laboratories or usable arms, no one in Washington seems to know or is willing to say.

Nasser Asad al-Tamimi, an Islamic radical, has been vocal. Early this year Al-Balad, a Jordanian newspaper, quoted him as saying that "jihad" had at last discovered how to win the holy war—lethal germs.

Disturbingly, growing interest abroad is shared by domestic radicals and militia groups at home. Catalogs catering to them carry ads for such books as "Guide to Germ Warfare." Larry Wayne Harris, an Ohioan with a history of hate-group affiliations, was arrested in 1995 for having bought plague bacteria from a germ bank under false pretenses. A registered microbiologist, he now says the microbes were strictly for defensive purposes.

"There are groups all over the world after this kind of stuff," Harris said, his blue eyes icy. "You're not going to stop germ warfare. The only thing to do is defend yourself."

The Assessment

Intelligence experts say knowing the truth is hard. Spies and satellites are only marginally helpful for ferreting out biological gear as small as kitchen cookware that is easy to hide and whose purpose can be peaceful (unlike the nuclear arms, bombers, ships, missiles and factories that dominated the Cold War). Even hundreds of arms inspectors in Iraq, who probed that nation for seven years, ended up with as many questions as answers.

Moreover, the attention focused on germ warfare has already helped give rise to germ hoaxes, and experts worry that serious concern might give way to complacency. This year, the FBI is fighting a wave of false anthrax threats in letters mailed to abortion clinics.

Federal officials note that Ramzi Ahmed Yousef, mastermind of the 1993 New York World Trade Center blast, which killed six people and injured more than 1,000, claimed that his goal was to have one tower fall into the other and kill a quarter million people—more than died in the atomic bombing of Hiroshima.

A top former official disclosed that Yousef, when arrested in 1995, was found to have been studying not only chemical but biological weapons.

John Gannon, chairman of the National Intelligence Council of the CIA, last month told a Stanford University meeting that the danger of germ and chemical devastation is rising.

He warned that terrorists and foes with such weapons are growing in number and that the increasingly lethal agents they are developing "have the potential to cause massive casualties."

The Response

Federal officials are struggling to tighten commerce in germs both at home and abroad. President Clinton himself recently raised the issue at Camp David with Brazilian President Fernando Henrique Cardoso, who has begun a program to restrict germ sales.

In Russia, Washington is expanding cooperative programs meant to keep former germ warriors in place doing peaceful research.

In NATO, Washington is arguing that the Atlantic alliance should take the lead in a global fight to stop terrorists from getting or using germ weaponry.

Meanwhile, the U.S. military is vaccinating all troops against anthrax, which causes high fevers and death, and has begun a $322 million program to build stockpiles of 18 other vaccines, including one against smallpox. Recently, Congress approved $51 million to start building domestic stockpiles of medicines and antibiotics, especially for police, fire and health workers.

Physical security at key federal buildings is being enhanced to foil terrorists who might try to spread deadly germs and chemicals through the air. The steps include ventilation improvements so a gentle breeze blows outward whenever a door or window is opened. In theory, this so-called positive pressure will automatically sweep away dangerous agents.

Across the country, federal officials are holding seminars in the nation's top 120 cities to train emergency personnel.

More broadly, intelligence agencies are struggling to monitor terrorists more closely. The FBI's nightmare is talented loners, who are difficult to track.

The Pentagon is weighing whether to ask the President to authorize appointment of a military commander who could plan and direct operations to defend the continental United States in the event of germ chaos, a step beyond the civil defenses of the early Cold War. No such commander's post now exists.

"Within minutes of an event, people are going to turn to us," Deputy Defense Secretary John Hamre told a meeting of military officials in explaining the need for homeland defense. "It could get crazy very fast."

To date, there has been little public debate over the risks and benefits of such actions, partly because the many responses to the germ threat have been both quiet, to avoid frightening Americans, and piecemeal.

But that may change as echoes of bomb shelters start to reverberate and as Washington scans the horizon to better judge the danger in the years and decades ahead.

Tension is sure to rise between the need for protection and "rights to privacy, something that we hold very dear," Defense Secretary William Cohen recently told the Council on Foreign Relations. That kind of friction, he added, will force "unpleasant choices" in the near future. "We haven't really faced up to it yet."

Exercise Finds U.S. Unable to Handle Germ War Threat[2]

On a bright spring day last month, 40 officials from more than a dozen Federal agencies met secretly near the White House to play out what would happen if terrorists attacked the United States with a devastating new type of germ weapon, Government officials say.

The results were not encouraging.

Under the scenario, terrorists spread a virus along the Mexican-American border, primarily in California and the southwest. After doctors diagnosed the epidemic as smallpox, the dreaded killer once thought to have been eradicated, vaccines were rushed in to immunize the population. But what appeared to have been smallpox turned out to be a hybrid whose hidden side caused profuse bleeding and a high fever for which there was no cure.

The United States, despite huge investments of time, money and effort in recent years, is still unprepared to respond to biological terror weapons.

As the scenario unfolded, officials playing the role of state and local officials were quickly overwhelmed by a panicked population, thousands of whom were falling ill and dying. Discovering huge gaps in logistics, legal authority and medical care, they began quarreling among themselves and with Washington over how to stem the epidemic. In truth, no one was in charge.

The outcome of the exercise surprised some participants but illustrated what others had long suspected: the United States, despite huge investments of time, money and effort in recent years, is still unprepared to respond to biological terror weapons.

The secret exercise, officials said, also underscored the need for a sweeping plan that President Clinton is expected to approve this week. The goal of the two new "Presidential decision directives," known as PDD-62 and PDD-63, is to enhance the country's ability to prevent chemical, biological or cyber-weapon attacks, and if deterrence fails, to respond more effectively to the mayhem.

Mr. Clinton's interest, especially in germ warfare, has been deepened by books, aides said. Mr. Clinton was so alarmed by one of them—a novel by Richard Preston titled *The Cobra Event* (Random House), which portrays a lone terrorist's

---

2. Article by Judith Miller and William J. Broad from the *New York Times*, I p1 Apr. 26, 1998. Copyright © 1998 the New York Times Company. Reprinted with permission.

attack on New York City with a genetically engineered virus—that he instructed intelligence experts to evaluate its credibility. Experts tend to disagree on the plausibility of such high-technology threats. But most agree that the danger will grow and that such an attack, if successful, could be catastrophic.

Administration officials said the President had become increasingly worried by the idea of germ-wielding terrorists who might cripple the nation by sowing deadly epidemics.

Mr. Clinton's personal interest, officials said, has become a powerful force behind a series of secret Federal meetings and directives meant to bolster the nation's anti-terrorism work. Mr. Clinton has also asked the National Security Council if more money is needed in this year's budget for anti-terrorism efforts.

During Mr. Clinton's presidency, terrorism has emerged as one of the country's thorniest security threats. In February 1993, a month after he took office, a terrorist bomb exploded under the World Trade Center in New York, killing 6 people and injuring 1,000.

In March 1995, a Japanese cult, Aum Shinrikyo, staged a stunning chemical attack on the Tokyo subway system, killing 12 and injuring 5,000. While the group used a lethal nerve gas, it turned out that it had also worked hard to make biological weapons, a realization that a senior Administration official characterized as a "wake-up call."

Then, in April 1995, terrorists blew up the Federal office building in Oklahoma City, killing 168 people.

Apprehension about germs grew later in 1995 as Iraq admitted that it had built and hidden a large biological arsenal and was prepared to use it during the Persian Gulf War in 1991.

On June 21, 1995, President Clinton signed PDD-39, which stated that the United States had "no higher priority" than stopping terrorists from acquiring weapons of mass destruction. More than 40 agencies vied for a piece of the new Federal pie, eager for part of the billions of dollars that Congress began appropriating for anti-terrorism programs.

The General Accounting Office, in a report last December, faulted the Government for a serious lack of coordination in efforts to counter the terrorist threat. For instance, it said there was no mechanism to prevent huge duplication of effort in some areas and inaction in others.

Richard A. Falkenrath, executive director of Harvard's Center for Science and International Affairs and author of *America's Achilles Heel* (The MIT Press), a new book on high-technology terrorism, also criticized the Government's efforts.

"There is still no overarching Federal blueprint for response," he said in an interview. "What you have now are mostly grass-roots efforts springing up in a wide range of agencies."

The Government concedes at least some of its failings. According to a draft of an interagency study, Government counterterrorism programs suffer from a lack of intelligence-sharing and a lack of information about what individual terrorists or groups may be plotting, the *Washington Post* reported Friday.

Government counterterrorism programs suffer from a lack of intelligence-sharing and a lack of information about what individual terrorists or groups may be plotting.

Last month's secret exercise, known as a table top, the civilian version of a military war game, used a genetically engineered virus—a mix of the smallpox and Marburg viruses.

Dr. William A. Haseltine, a leading expert on genetic engineering whom the White House asked to review the scenario, said in an interview that it was realistic. "You could make such a virus today," he said. "Any trained molecular virologist with a really good lab can do it."

But Dr. John W. Huggins, head of viral therapies at the United States Army Medical Research Institute of Infectious Diseases at Fort Detrick, Md., disagreed. "Most of us think it's many years away," he said, adding, though, that using the conjectural hybrid in a worst-case Federal exercise made sense.

Administration officials said the scenario was purposely intended to inflict a substantial disaster so as to stress the system and reveal weakness in emergency preparedness.

Among the shortcomings that were discovered, officials said, were that hospitals quickly exhausted supplies of antibiotics and vaccine. One participant said that it was very hard "to get trained, immunized medical staff into an infected area."

Federal quarantine laws turned out to be too antiquated to deal with the crisis, and almost no state had serious plans for how to take care of the people it had isolated.

Plus, what began as a domestic disaster rapidly spiraled into an international crisis as the epidemic threatened to spread into Mexico.

President Clinton's deepening interest in such potential threats, aides said, led him to request a briefing by a panel of experts this month on the genetic engineering of biological weapons and related issues.

For 90 minutes on April 10, he questioned seven scientists and Cabinet members about what a White House statement described as "opportunities and the national security challenges posed by genetic engineering and biotechnology."

"Although he had been up most of the previous night helping settle the Irish crisis, he was very engaged and asked probing questions," said Frank Young, former head of the Food and Drug Administration, who campaigned for better emergency preparedness when in government and who moderated the panel.

Others present said Mr. Clinton had asked the experts for written advice on how to detect and deter the consequences of a biological attack.

Dr. Young, now a pastor and executive director of the Reformed Theological Seminary, Metro Washington, declined to discuss the panel's recommendations, which are expected to be submitted this week.

But those familiar with the report said the panel had urged Mr. Clinton, among other things, to stockpile and develop the capacity to rapidly make antidotes, vaccines and antibiotics, adopt a system to verify that states are observing the 1972 treaty banning biological weapons, increase Federal funds for drug and medical research, strengthen the public-health sector and streamline the Government system for detecting and managing biological crises.

Last Wednesday, senior officials told a joint Senate hearing that the Administration might create a national stockpile of vaccines, antibiotics and antidotes to save lives in the event of a chemical or biological attack by terrorists.

The improvements in organization that President Clinton is poised to endorse had provoked a bitter fight within the Administration, with the Departments of Defense and Justice opposing a key provision that critics feared would have created a terrorism czar within the White House. Instead, the directives now create a "national coordinator" with a limited staff and no direct budget authority, but wide powers to initiate action, secure aid, and iron out Government disputes.

The job is expected to go to Richard A. Clarke, now President Clinton's special assistant for global affairs. His new role will be to strengthen efforts to foil terrorists intent on killing Americans or destroying the nation's "critical infrastructure"—the maze of private and public institutions that provide power, money, water, transportation, communications, and health services.

Under the system mandated by the new Presidential directives, as described by Administration officials, combating terrorism is divided into 10 areas: apprehension and prosecution, disruptions abroad, international cooperation, preventing weapon acquisition, crisis management, transportation security, critical infrastructure, government continuity, countering foreign threats domestically and protection of Americans abroad.

President Steps Up War on New Terrorism[3]

WASHINGTON, Jan. 22—President Clinton proposed steps today to defend against unconventional terrorist warfare, including creation of 25 urban medical emergency teams to respond to germ weapons attacks and the training of a new Cyber Corps of computer specialists to detect and defeat intrusions into critical civilian and military computer networks.

In an address at the National Academy of Sciences, Mr. Clinton sought to muster public support for a large increase in Federal spending to combat exotic threats. He said that terrorists with computer skills and access to chemical and biological agents had extended the field of battle from physical space to cyberspace and from land, sea and air to the human body.

The President's proposals stand a good chance of passage on Capitol Hill, where Republican lawmakers have been pressing for several years to strengthen Federal counterterrorism programs.

Mr. Clinton said that the Department of Health and Human Services was being enlisted in the battle against domestic terrorism, expanding its disease-fighting role into a national security mission. The agency will be charged with developing and stockpiling vaccines and treatments against chemical and germ weapons and with mobilizing public health agencies to respond to any suspected attack of infectious agents.

The President's actions are a significant expansion of Federal involvement in efforts to respond to threats that officials say are quickly moving from the realm of science fiction to reality. Mr. Clinton said that defenses against unconventional threats had failed to keep pace with the speed of development of new kinds of weapons of terror, weapons that can be developed in a clandestine laboratory and transported in a briefcase or sent through the mail.

Mr. Clinton also warned that a talented hacker with a desktop computer and a modem could now threaten the nation's military, banking, communications, power, transportation and water networks.

Clinton . . . said that terrorists with computer skills and access to chemical and biological agents had extended the field of battle from physical space to cyberspace and from land, sea and air to the human body.

---

3. Article by John M. Broder from the *New York Times* A p14 Jan. 23, 1999. Copyright © 1999 the New York Times Company. Reprinted with permission.

"All of you know the fight against terrorism is far from over, and now terrorists seek new tools of destruction," Mr. Clinton told Government officials and scientists today. "The enemies of peace realize they cannot defeat us with traditional military means, so they are working on two new forms of assault which you've heard about today: cyberattacks on our critical computer systems, and attacks with weapons of mass destruction—chemical, biological, potentially even nuclear weapons."

Mr. Clinton sought to increase awareness of emerging threats without raising undue alarm about events that have yet to materialize on American soil. He said the Government would assure civil liberties even as it organized its military, intelligence, criminal justice and public health agencies to respond to the threat of biological or computer terrorism.

"This is not a cause for panic," Mr. Clinton said today. "It is essential that we do not undermine liberty in the name of liberty. We can prevail over terrorism by drawing on the very best in our free society: the skill and courage of our troops, the genius of our scientists and engineers, the strength of our factory workers, the determination and talents of our public servants, the vision of leaders in every vital sector."

Mr. Clinton's plan devotes $2.8 billion to prepare for attacks with exotic weapons and to combat computer warfare threats.

Over the last two years, the Administration has almost doubled the money devoted to protecting Americans against attacks with unconventional weapons.

Over the last two years, the Administration has almost doubled the money devoted to protecting Americans against attacks with unconventional weapons. The President's 2000 budget proposal allocates $1.4 billion.

Included in the total are $683 million to train emergency workers in American cities to cope with a chemical attack or an outbreak of bioterrorism; $206 million to protect Government sites; $381 million for research on pathogens, development of vaccines and therapies, technology to detect and diagnose rare illnesses, and decontamination.

The White House is also requesting $87 million, a 23 percent increase over current spending, to improve the nation's public health surveillance system to better detect the outbreak of an epidemic and determine if it is an act of nature or of deliberate terror.

The proposal also includes $52 million to continue to build a national stockpile of specialized medicines to protect civilians against attack by germ agents like anthrax, smallpox or pneumonic plague. The Administration is also seeking to triple spending, to $24 million, to create 25 new urban medical response teams in major American cities. Only four cities—Miami, Denver, Washington, and Charlotte, N.C.—have teams prepared to respond to a biological or chemical weapons emergency.

"We're all here talking about a kind of scenario that we hope that our citizens never have to confront, but the point is to be prepared," said Donna E. Shalala, the Secretary of Health and Human Services, who appeared with Mr. Clinton today. "This is the first time in American history in which the public health system has been integrated directly into the national security system."

The other half of the President's proposal is an intensified effort to protect the nation's critical, computer-based infrastructure—from power grids to firefighting networks. Such defenses have seen a 40 percent spending increase in the last two years, from slightly less than $1 billion in 1998 to the more than $1.46 billion being sought for fiscal year 2000.

Much of that money will go to the Pentagon for development of systems that detect unauthorized intrusion into sensitive computer networks. The Administration also proposes to spend $500 million for research on preventing efforts by computer hackers to disrupt and damage Government and private information networks.

The Administration budget proposal also includes money to create a "Cyber Corps," a cadre of computer security experts who can respond to a computer crisis. The White House said it would spend several million dollars next year to begin to design a program to train and recruit computer science students as a counter-hacker squad.

While these numbers appear small given the Government's huge budget, Administration officials noted today that the money will significantly accelerate research on biological weapons agents and the means to treat them.

Representative Curt Weldon, Republican of Pennsylvania, said he was pleased that Mr. Clinton was devoting attention and money to a problem he has sought to publicize for years.

"Congress has been been the one to take the initiative on the issue, while the Clinton Administration has largely ignored these threats," said Mr. Weldon, chairman of the research and development subcommittee of the House Armed Services Committee. "It's good to see that the President has finally come around; better late than never."

Senate Raps Investigation, Chemical Warfare Training[4]

A new Senate report criticizes the federal investigation of Gulf War illnesses but generally supports findings suggesting there's no single cause of the illnesses.

Moreover, most military units are not adequately trained to respond to future chemical or biological attacks, the report said.

"There is no smoking gun in this report, no explosive new evidence that says 'whodunit' and why," committee member Sen. Robert Byrd said. But the report confirms that veterans were exposed to "a poison cocktail of hazardous materials, that many are now ill, and that the bureaucratic response has been slow and stumbling," Byrd said.

The report concluded that the U.S. military was not adequately prepared to deal with the threat of biological or chemical warfare and is still unprepared today.

The DoD investigation didn't integrate crucial weather information provided by the Air Force, according to the Sept. 1 report from the special investigation unit of the Senate Veterans' Affairs Committee. Neither did the department subject its findings to important critical scientific review by outside experts, the report said.

A scientific consultant contracted by the Senate investigators supported these criticisms. The consultant also said DoD grossly overestimated the numbers of service members who may have been exposed to chemical warfare agents.

The investigating unit found no evidence to either prove or disprove Iraq used chemical weapons during the Gulf War.

However, the report concluded that the U.S. military was not adequately prepared to deal with the threat of biological or chemical warfare and is still unprepared today.

"Although the threat of chemical and biological warfare has increased since the Gulf War and hangs heavy over the potential battlefields of the 21st century, the military still has inadequate supplies of vaccines and chemical biological protective equipment," the report said.

"Almost eight years after the Gulf War, our military is still not prepared to fight in a chemical or biological warfare environment," said committee member Sen. Jay Rockefeller. The senator pointed to a DoD inspector general report that corroborates these findings.

---

4. Article by the American Forces Press Service for *National Guard* magazine p18 + Oct. 1998. Copyright © 1998 *National Guard* magazine. Reprinted with permission.

Bernard Rostker, who heads the DoD Gulf War illness investigation, said the Senate report contains good insight about the investigation and recommendations for improvement.

He said his investigation revealed a need for better record-keeping, medical surveillance, environmental sampling and forward-deploying biological detection. Since the Gulf War, he said, DoD has fielded a new gas mask, tested medical dog tags and begun developing improved chemical alarm systems.

"I can't take direct credit, but the importance of these issues is consistent with what we have learned," he said.

DoD also has launched a department wide vaccination program that eventually will provide every service member and certain civilian employees and contractors with protection against anthrax, a deadly nerve agent that can be easily weaponized.

Anyone deploying to the Persian Gulf receives the shots, and those assigned to units in South Korea received the first of a series of six required inoculations in September.

The New Terror Fear: Biological Weapons[5]

America is stepping up preparations to cope with biological warfare. This month, at undisclosed locations in Denver, medical and weapons experts will begin to assess the city's ability to contend with terrorists using biological, radiological, or chemical weapons of mass destruction. Denver is the first of 120 cities where federal authorities will evaluate emergency capabilities under a $42.6 million Domestic Preparedness Program that is the largest civil defense initiative since the Cold War. This program begins two weeks after the Pentagon granted the first contract in a possible $400 million program to develop a detection system to sniff out deadly airborne microbes spread by an enemy.

Three events have created the new urgency: Iraq deployed missiles bearing anthrax germs, botulinum (a toxin that spreads the deadly disease botulism), and aflatoxin (a poison derived from mold) during the 1991 Persian Gulf war, and its biological weapons program continues, according to intelligence experts; a 1995 Tokyo attack in which the cult-like terrorist group Aum spread nerve gas in the subway system killing 12 people; and a little-publicized conviction in Ohio last month of a microbiologist named Larry Wayne Harris, who pleaded guilty to fraudulently obtaining bubonic plague cultures. Harris, who has ties to right-wing groups, was sentenced to 18 months probation and community service. The plague cultures were obtained by Harris with such ease that in 1996 Congress tightened laws on commerce in deadly biological materials to make sure they were ordered for legitimate medical and scientific purposes.

Poor man's nukes. The CIA now says Iraq has been joined by North Korea, Iran, Libya, Syria, and even China in the quest to make biological weapons. Their motive is simple: Biologicals are cheaper and easier to make than nuclear or chemical weapons, and they can be equally as devastating. The U.S. Office of Technology Assessment once estimated that a small private plane, with 220 pounds of anthrax spores, flying over Washington on a clear, windless night,

5. Article by Nicholas Horrock for *U.S. News & World Report* p36 May 12, 1997. Copyright © 1997 *U.S. News and World Report*. Reprinted with permission. Visit us at our Web site at www.usnews.com for additional information.

could trail an invisible, odorless mist that would kill between 1 million and 3 million people.

However, retired Army Col. Karl Lowe, an arms-control expert, argued in a recent essay that it would be very hard for terrorists to carry off a biological attack. Many biologicals can be dissipated by wind or rain, or must be ingested in such enormous amounts as to make their use as a weapon of mass destruction impossible.

Though difficult to execute, a biological attack would be virtually impossible to detect in its early stages. "Ideally we would like to develop a detection system using something remote, like a laser beam that could detect and identify a biological agent at standoff distances," says Assistant Defense Secretary Harold Smith. But that prospect is years away, so the Pentagon is trying to develop a "point detector" that could be mounted on a remote-controlled vehicle. It should be able to sniff air samples and determine within 15 minutes whether any of 26 dangerous agents are present, according to Brig. Gen. John Doesburg, whose command awarded the first contract for such a vehicle last month.

The best detector now is a Humvee mounted with what appears to be a small Hansel and Gretel house with three chimneys, named in the Army's cumbersome fashion the Biological Integrated Detection System, or BIDS. The problem with BIDS is that it takes two persons to operate, requires 30 to 45 minutes to identify biological agents (an eternity in combat), and can simultaneously identify only four. Next year, DOD will field a temporary improvement, the Air Base/Port Biological Detection system, at bases in two areas of high tension, like South Korea and Saudi Arabia.

On the civilian side, a law passed last year requires DOD to go beyond troop protection and assist in civil defense. An incident in Washington, D.C., last month added urgency to the effort. The headquarters of the B'nai B'rith, the national Jewish service organization, received a package with a threatening note and the laboratory words for anthrax on it. It turned out to be harmless, but had anthrax been loose in Washington's downtown, U.S. readiness would have faced the supreme test.

Though difficult to execute, a biological attack would be virtually impossible to detect in its early stages.

Appendix I: Chemical Weapons Chronology[a]

Since 1980, the Council For A Livable World Education Fund has designed programs to educate the public about nuclear weapons, the dangers of the arms race, and the search for peaceful alternatives. In addition to a briefing book series, Education Fund projects produce timely fact sheets and newsletters for use by the arms control community, work the media on the issues, and provide briefings for policy makers and their staff. The entries on this timeline from 1915 to 1996 appeared on the Council for a Livable World Education Fund Web site. The entries from 1997 to 1999 have been added by the editor.

1915 - First use of chemical warfare in World War I, with the German use of chlorine gas at Ypres, Belgium. Total estimated casualties on all sides from chemical warfare in World War I are estimated at 1.3 million.

1925 - Negotiation of Geneva Protocol which bars use of chemical weapons in wartime.

1935 - Italians use chemical weapons against Ethiopia.

Late 1930's - Japanese use chemical weapons in China.

World War II - Chemical weapons were not used.

1968 - Negotiations begin in Geneva on a treaty banning chemical weapons.

1969 - President Richard Nixon orders a moratorium on U.S. chemical weapons production and renounced possession of all forms of germ and toxin weaponry.

1972 - General discussion on a chemical weapons ban begin within the multinational U.N. Committee on Disarmament in Geneva.

1975 - Congress bars moves to resume new chemical weapons production.

1976 - President Gerald Ford launches bilateral negotiations on a chemical ban.

1980 - Congress appropriates the first funds for a new nerve gas facility in Pine Bluff, Arkansas.

1982 - President Reagan makes a formal request to resume production of nerve gas weapons; Congress rejected the request in 1982, 1983 and 1984.

1984 - Vice President George Bush presents in Geneva, Switzerland, a new draft chemical weapons treaty.

1985 - Congress approves production of binary chemical weapons.

1987 - The first new chemical weapons produced by the United States in 18 years rolls off the assembly line.

1988 - Iraqi government uses poison gas to kill an estimated 4,000 people of its own people in the Kurdish village of Halabja.

1989 - Seventy-five Senators sign a letter to President Bush urging completion of a chemical weapons treaty.

---

a. From the Council for a Livable World Education Fund Web site. Copyright © Council for a Livable World Education Fund.

1989 - U.S. and U.S.S.R. sign Wyoming Memorandum of Understanding for bilateral verification experiments on verifying a chemical ban and a data exchange on stockpiles.

1990 - U.S. and U.S.S.R. sign an agreement to stop producing chemical weapons and to reduce their chemical weapons stockpiles to no more than 5,000 agent tons by the end of 2002 (later extended to 2004).

1991 - Iraqi President Saddam Hussein threatens to use chemical weapons in the Persian Gulf War, but refrains from doing so.

1992 - Chemical Weapons Convention completed in Geneva and approved by the United Nations.

1993 - The Bush Administration, joining 129 other countries, signs the Chemical Weapons Convention in Paris.

1993 - President Clinton on November 23 formally submits the Chemical Weapons Convention to the Senate for its advice and consent.

1994 - Sen. Jesse Helms blocks action on the Chemical Weapons Convention in the waning days of the 103rd Congress.

1995 - Senate unanimous consent agreement in December to complete action on the Chemical Weapons Convention no later than April 30, 1996.

1996 - Discovery of secret Libyan deep underground chemical weapons production facility, which the Pentagon estimates could be finished in a year's time.

1996 - Senate Foreign Relations Committee votes 1-5 in favor of a resolution of ratification on April 25, 1996.

1996 - Senate unanimous consent agreement to bring Chemical Weapons Convention to a vote prior to September 14, 1996.

1996 - Senate postpones consideration of the Convention in the heat of the Presidential campaign in September 1996.

1997 - The Chemical Weapons Convention goes into effect on April 29, with inspectors being sent out to monitor compliance.

1997 - As of November, Saddam Hussein bans United Nations inspectors from entering Iraqi sites suspected of containing chemical as well as biological weapons.

1998 - A September 1 Senate report assesses U.S. ability to cope with chemical and biological attack, and criticizes the federal government for its handling of Gulf War syndrome.

1999 - President Clinton calls for the allocation of $2.8 billion to defend against chemical weapons and other forms of "unconventional" terrorist strikes, in an address to the National Academy of Sciences on January 2.

1999 - A three-day conference of scientists, doctors, and politicians is conducted in Atlanta, Georgia, from February 28 to March 2, on the subject of Gulf War syndrome.

Appendix II: CDSP Site Locations[a]

The Chemical Stockpile Disposal Program (CSDP) was established to oversee chemical weapons disposal as part of the U.S. Army's program to destroy its entire stockpile of chemical weapons by the year 2007 (in compliance with the Chemical Weapons Convention). Weapons are currently stored at eight sites in the continental United States and at Johnston Island in the Pacific Ocean. The following location states are highlighted on the map below:

- Anniston Chemical Activity (ANCA) - Anniston, Alabama (New Content)
- Blue Grass Chemical Activity (BGCA) - Richmond, Kentucky (New Content)
- Deseret Chemical Depot (DCD) - Tooele, Utah (New Content)
- Edgewood Chemical Activity (ECA) - Aberdeen Proving Ground, Maryland
- Johnston Atoll (JACADS) - 825 miles southwest of Hawaii
- Newport Chemical Depot (NECD) - Newport, Indiana
- Pine Bluff Chemical Activity (PBCA) - Pine Bluff, Arkansas (New Content)
- Pueblo Chemical Depot (PUCD) - Pueblo, Colorado
- Umatilla Chemical Depot (UMCD) - Hermiston, Oregon (New Content)

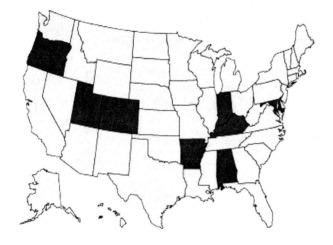

---

a. Map from U.S. Army. Reprinted with permission. This map and other information on the CDSP can be found online at http://www-pmcd.apgea.army.mil.

Bibliography

Books and Pamphlets

Alibek, Ken; Handelman, Stephen. *Biohazard: The Chilling True Story of the Largest Covert Biological Weapons Program in the World–Told from the Inside by the Man Who Ran It.* Random House, 1999.

Bernauer, Thomas. *The Chemistry of Regime Formation: Explaining International Cooperation for a Comprehensive Ban on Chemical Weapons.* Dartmouth Pub. Co., 1993.

Bernauer, Thomas; United Nations Institute for Disarmament Research. *The Projected Chemical Weapons Convention: A Guide to the Negotiations in the Conference on Disarmament.* United Nations, 1990.

Carus, W. Seth. "The Poor Man's Atomic Bomb?": Biological Weapons in the Middle East. Washington Inst. for Near East Policy, 1991.

Chow, Brian G.; United States Air Force. *Air Force Operations in a Chemical and Biological Environment.* Rand Corp., 1998.

Cole, Leonard A. *The Eleventh Plague: The Politics of Biological and Chemical Warfare.* W. H. Freeman, 1997.

Cordesman, Anthony H. *Weapons of Mass Destruction in the Middle East.* Brassey's, 1991.

Croddy, Eric. *Chemical and Biological Warfare: An Annotated Bibliography.* Scarecrow Press, 1997.

Crone, Hugh D. *Banning Chemical Weapons: The Scientific Background.* Cambridge Univ. Press, 1992.

Dando, Malcolm. *Biological Warfare in the 21st Century: Biotechnology and the Proliferation of Biological Weapons.* Brassey's, 1994.

Dorn, A. Walter; United Nations Institute for Disarmament Research. *Index to the Chemical Weapons Convention.* United Nations, 1993.

Douglass, Joseph D; Livingstone, Neil C. *America the vulnerable: the threat of chemical and biological warfare.* Lexington Bks., 1987.

Forsberg, Randall. *Nonproliferation Primer: Preventing the Spread of Nuclear, Chemical, and Biological Weapons.* MIT Press, 1995.

Johnson, Stuart E., ed; National Defense University Institute for National Strategic Studies. *The Niche Threat: Deterring the Use of Chemical and Biological Weapons.* National Defense Univ. Press, 1997.

Krutzsch, Walter; Trapp, Ralf. A *Commentary on the Chemical Weapons Convention.* Nijhoff, M., 1994.

Lundin, S. J., ed.; Stockholm International Peace Research Institute. *Views on Possible Verification Measures for the Biological Weapons Convention.* Oxford Univ. Press, 1991.

Mauroni, Albert J. *Chemical Biological Defense: U.S. Military Policies and Decisions in the Gulf War.* Praeger Pubs., 1998.

McCuen, Gary E., ed. *Poison in the Wind: The Spread of Chemical and Biological Weapons.* McCuen Publs., 1992.

Morel, Benoit, ed.; Olson, Kyle B., ed. *Shadows and Substance: The Chemical Weapons Convention.* Westview Press, 1993.

Pringle, Laurence P. *Chemical and Biological Warfare: The Cruelest Weapons.* Enslow Pubs., 1993.

Ranger, Robin; Wiencek, David G. *The Devil's Brews II: Weapons of Mass Destruction and International Security.* University of Lancaster. Centre for Defence and Int. Security Studies, 1997.

Sims, Nicholas Roger Alan. *The Diplomacy of Biological Disarmament: Vicissitudes of a Treaty in Force, 1975–85.* St. Martin's Press, 1988.

Roberts, Brad, ed. *Ratifying the Chemical Weapons Convention.* Center for Strategic and Int. Studies, 1994.

Roberts, Brad, ed. *Biological Weapons: Weapons of the Future?* Center for Strategic and Int. Studies, 1993.

Stock, Thomas, ed.; Sutherland, Ronald G., ed.; Stockholm International Peace Research Institute. *National Implementation of the Future Chemical Weapons Convention.* Oxford Univ. Press, 1990.

Trapp, Ralf. *Verification under the Chemical Weapons Convention: On Site Inspection in Chemical Industry Facilities.* Oxford Univ. Press, 1993.

Zilinskas, Raymond A., ed. *The Microbiologist and Biological Defense Research: Ethics, Politics, and International Security.* New York Acad. of Sciences, 1992.

Additional Periodical Articles with Abstracts

Readers interested in learning more about chemical and biological warfare may refer to the articles listed below. Please note that some of the articles listed reflect issues not addressed in this book, and are intended to help readers broaden their knowledge of contemporary issues associated with chemical and biological warfare.

AMC and the CWC. Henry, Celia. *Analytical Chemistry.* v. 70 no7 p. 246A Ap 1 '98

The Army Materiel Command (AMC) Treaty Laboratory in Edgewood, Maryland, is profiled. The AMC Treaty Laboratory is the only laboratory on the American continent to succeed consistently in round-robin proficiency tests with Chemical Weapons Convention (CWC)-type materials. Under the CWC, any necessary analyses must be performed on site, the AMC Treaty Laboratory has created compact, rugged modular laboratories that can be whisked to locations across the globe. The laboratory, which was accredited by the International Organization of Standardization, is also involved in cooperative research and development agreements, or CRADAs.

The U.S. as a "Hot Zone": the Necessity for Medical Defense. Eppright, Charles T. *Armed Forces and Society.* 25:37-58 Fall '98

This article calls for awareness of the national security threat to the United States from "emerging disease" and ultimately suggests a response mechanism based upon existing government resources, which the author calls "medical defense." National security strategy is analyzed in the context of recognition of nontraditional threats in the midst of the "Revolution in Security Affairs." Relevant governmental scientific strategies concerning emerging diseases are examined in order to develop the medical defense concept. The article further outlines the problem of medical defense in the format of threat, scenario, and mission analyses. Threat analysis concentrates on how deteriorating social and political conditions are enhancing the environment of emerging disease. Scenario analysis focuses on the effects of an attack from an emerging disease, with discussion of the deficiencies present in the U.S. public health system. Mission analysis demonstrates how the U.S. could prepare an adequate medical defense by aligning specialized military medical capability with those of the Centers for Disease Control. Finally, the formation, mission, and command and control of a military unit formed specifically for medical defense are outlined. Reprinted by permission of the publisher.

Bioterrorism as a Public Health Threat. McDade, Joseph E; Franz, David. *Emerging Infectious Diseases.* v. 4 no3 p. 493-4 Jy-S '98

Part of a special issue devoted to the proceedings of the International Conference on Emerging Infectious Diseases on March 8-11. The public health aspects of bioterrorism are discussed. Bioterrorist attacks could be covert or announced and could be due to virtually any microorganism. The attack might be difficult to distinguish from naturally occurring outbreaks of infection, but clues could be obtained from the etiology and epidemiology of the outbreak. Public health officials need to be fully aware that infectious disease outbreaks could be due to bioterrorism, and maintenance of effective disease surveillance is an essential component of preparedness. Collaboration between the various agencies and organizations such as the CDC and the FBI is essential to ensure that the U.S. is ready to deal with bioterrorist attacks.

Bioterrorism as a Public Health Threat. Henderson, D. A. *Emerging Infectious Diseases*. v. 4 no3 p. 488-92 Jy-S '98

The threat of bioterrorism, long ignored and denied, has heightened over the past few years. Recent events in Iraq, Japan, and Russia cast an ominous shadow. Two candidate agents are of special concern--smallpox and anthrax. The magnitude of the problems and the gravity of the scenarios associated with release of these organisms have been vividly portrayed by two epidemics of smallpox in Europe during the 1970s and by an accidental release of aerosolized anthrax from a Russian bioweapons facility in 1979. Efforts in the United States to deal with possible incidents involving bioweapons in the civilian sector have only recently begun and have made only limited progress. Only with substantial additional resources at the federal, state, and local levels can a credible and meaningful response be mounted. For longer-term solutions, the medical community must educate both the public and policy makers about bioterrorism and build a global consensus condemning its use. Reprinted by permission of the publisher

Super Sponges. Medlin, Jennifer F., *Environmental Health Perspectives*. v. 106 no 4 p. A182-184 Ag '98

Two scientists based in Pittsburgh, Pennsylvania, have developed an enzyme-infused sponge that could be used to detoxify harmful chemicals. Keith E. LeJeune of Carnegie Mellon University and Alan J. Russell of the University of Pittsburgh immobilized phosphodiesterase in a matrix of polyurethane foam. Once tethered, the enzyme becomes stable at room temperature and retains high activity for a long period of time. This system could find application in removing nerve agents from the skin and clothing of soldiers exposed to chemical weapons and in sponging off pesticides from agricultural or industrial workers. The foam could also be used to clean surfaces or even, in liquid form, to decontaminate larger areas.

The Threat of Things Biological. VanderMeer, Dan C. *Environmental Health Perspectives*. v. 106 no6 p. A280-A282 Je '98

Biological threats and the way in which they can be addressed are discussed. The biological threats facing the world today include previously unknown infections such as the Ebola virus, HIV/AIDS, Lyme and Legionnaires' diseases, and deadly new strains of E. coli and Staphylococcus bacteria. Other threats are bacterial resistance to antibiotics and the development of biological warfare agents. Scientists, public health officials, policy makers, governments, and the public are trying to determine how to predict the spread of emerging infectious diseases and how to protect against their effects. Decisions must be made regarding which threats are the most urgent, how funding should be distributed for control and research, how to provide advice, how to establish health priorities, and how to design interventions to deal with the hazards.

Chemical Weapons Dilemma. Bailey, Kathleen. *Issues in Science and Technology*. v. 14 no3 p. 14 + Spring '98

In "Stay the Course on Chemical Weapons Ban" in the Winter 1997-98 Issues in Science and Technology, Amy E. Smithson disapproves of providing the U.S. president with authority to place U.S. security interests above the obligations of arms control treaties. The writer discusses Smithson's essay.

Emerging Infections on Center Stage at First Major International Meeting. Stephenson, Joan. *JAMA*. v. 279 no14 p. 1055-6 A 8 '98

The rising rates of nosocomial infections and other trends were discussed at the first large-scale international meeting on emerging infections, held last month in Atlanta, Georgia. Nosocomial infections have risen sharply nationwide in the past 20 years, and up to 70 percent of infections are resistant to one or more antibiotics. Experts pointed to a need for better surveillance and control of food-borne infections, and it was suggested that hidden pathogens such as Toxoplasma gondii are routinely missed. Diligence is also necessary with respect to new sources of food-borne microbes, and it was noted that control measures such as washing fresh produce or pasteurizing might not be enough to prevent disease. Finally, concern was expressed that the U.S. is ill prepared to cope with biological weapons such as smallpox and anthrax.

RAID Teams to Respond to Terrorism Threat. Gunby, Phil. *JAMA*. v. 279 no23 p. 1855 Je 17 '98

The Department of Defense is introducing RAID (rapid assessment and initial detection) teams to deal with possible attacks by terrorists and criminals who might use unconventional weapons of mass destruction. The teams will carry out first-response decontamination, treatment, and evacuation of exposed persons, and they will also determine whatever additional resources are needed. Some members will be involved in controlling panic, securing the area, and ensuring that communications remain open. A team will be established in each of the 10 Federal Emergency Management Agency regions, and the plan is to be phased in over the next 5 years, with the possibility of more teams in the future.

Biological Weapons: What Role Should Environmental Health Specialists Take in Protecting Our Communities? Wiant, Chris J. *Journal of Environmental Health*. v. 60 no9 p. 25 + My '98

The role of environmental health professionals in protecting communities against biological weapons is discussed. Although there have been few incidents in which biological weapons have been employed as offensive weapons of war or terrorism, they nevertheless pose a real threat. In the event of a terrorist attack in the U.S. using such weapons, it is likely that local emergency response will involve environmental health professionals, especially those who have been trained in disease investigation and in responding to hazardous materials incidents. The unique characteristics of biological agents make the general population vulnerable and necessitate a proactive response to the threat posed by such agents. In addition, public information support is crucial, particularly to manage the high levels of emotion or even panic that will certainly accompany a terrorist attack.

Creating the Faith: the Canadian Gas Services in the First World War. Cook, Tim. *Journal of Military History*. 62:755-86 O '98

The writer discusses the innovations of the Canadian Corps in coping with the evolution of poison gas. The development of a defensive gas doctrine, and the constant adaptation and training to a threat that became commonplace, ensured that the Canadian Corps remained an effective fighting force in the First World War. The Canadian response to the ever-expanding gas war was the eventual creating of the Canadian Corps Gas Services, which, once an efficient gas mask had been developed, taught such difficult tasks as how to use the mask, how to identify various poisonous gases and their harmless substitutes, and how as a consequence to adjust one's mask effectively. The Canadian structure was based on the British, but the self-contained nature of the Canadian Corps meant that speedier and more effective reforms could be introduced. Consequently, the Canadians, in relative terms, suffered considerably fewer gas casualties than the British Corps alongside whom they served, and, more importantly, by mid-1917 they could continue fighting and carrying out their unofficial role as shock troops.

Biological Warfare. Nass, Meryl. *Lancet*. v. 352 no9126 p. 491 2 Ag 8 '98

A letter responds to the May 9 article by Wise on bioterrorism. The writer points out that there is no person-to-person spread of anthrax, although anthrax can recur unpredictably in the future from a soil reservoir. Some points regarding the use of vaccines and other therapies in response to threats of biological warfare are discussed.

Slow Progress Made on Control of Biological Weapons. McGregor, Alan. *Lancet* v. 352 no9123 p. 209 Jl 18 '98

Negotiations to regulate compliance with the 1972 Biological Weapons Convention are progressing, albeit slowly. The recent session in Geneva, Switzerland, ended with a 250-page "rolling" text containing about 3,000 reservations from the participating countries. Further meetings are scheduled in September, but the chance of an agreed text before 1999 seems small.

USA Plans Major Effort to Counter Biowarfare. McCarthy,-Michael. *Lancet*. v. 351 no9116 p. 1641 My 30 '98

Major efforts are underway in the U.S. to counter the threat of biological warfare. On May 22, in a speech to the graduating class of the U.S. Naval Academy, President Clinton announced that the U.S. plans to make major moves to counter high-technology attacks on civilian populations using biological and chemical warfare agents. This effort will consist of the improvement of existing public health and medical surveillance systems, the preparation and equipment of local biowarfare emergency response personnel, the stockpiling of vaccines and medicines, and the establishment of a coordinated RandD effort.

Alleged Chemical Warfare in Bosnia Conflict. Sharp, David. *Lancet*. v. 351 no9114 p. 1500 My 16 '98

Extracts from interviews conducted by Alistair Hay with 35 survivors of a march from a village near the Bosnian town of Srebrenica during the Bosnian conflict appear in the May issue of Medicine, Conflict, and Survival. The object of these interviews was to explore a suggestion that there might be a connection between the hallucinations that were frequently reported by people on this march and the suspected use of chemical warfare. However, as Hay himself admits, a forensic chemical analysis of clothing found on a mountain where shelling was especially severe has revealed no trace of the atropine-like compound 3-quinuclidinyl benzilate (BZ).

Bioterrorism: Thinking the Unthinkable. Wise, Richard. *Lancet* v. 351 no9113 p. 1378 My 9 '98

The potential threat of biological warfare waged by terrorists is discussed. The sarin nerve gas attack in Tokyo, Japan, 4 years ago, changed perspectives about the potential threat of urban terrorism. The biological agents that could be employed by terrorists include anthrax, brucella, yersinia, francisella, Coxiella burnetii, Burkholderia, botulinum toxins, and smallpox. As a means of safeguarding against these potential threats, 140 countries have signed the Biological Weapons Convention of 1975; however, several Middle Eastern states have not. Clearly, there is a need for military and police intelligence and firm links with the medical community. If the threat of bioterrorism is to be faced, realistic plans and steps for preparedness must be developed.

From Mustard Gas to Biowarfare: Congress Tackles Military Medicine. Glass, Nigel. *Lancet*. v. 351 no9112 p. 1340 My 2 '98

The 32nd Congress of the International Committee on Military Medicine was held last week in Vienna, Austria. A range of issues were addressed at the meeting, including the nightmare scenarios of biological warfare, the incidence of traumatic stress disorders, and the detection of mustard gas and treatment of the injuries it causes. The health needs of civilians, who are increasingly caught up in conflicts, were also discussed.

Above All, Do No Harm: Noting J. B. S. Haldane's Pro-Chemical Warfare Thesis Callinicus. Gould, Stephen Jay. *Natural History*. v107 no8:16+ O '98

The inability to predict the future is one of the greatest ineptitudes of humans. Two obstacles generally stand in the way of successful prediction: People, in principle, cannot know much about complex futures along the pathways of history, and their views are motivated by social and personal prejudices, even though they think they are acting in a rational manner. Exercising moral restraint may be the only sure way of protecting the world from the unforeseen consequences of our actions. To highlight the danger of mixing scientific arrogance and flawed assumptions, the writer discusses the career of J. B. S. Haldane, a founder of modern evolutionary biology who advocated the use of chemical warfare even though the consequences of chemical weapons had not been fully explored.

First Shots Fired in Biological Warfare. Wheelis, Mark. *Nature*. v. 395 no6699 p. 213 S 17 '98

A letter comments on the recent report by Redmond et al. (1998;393:747-8) on plans by Germany to attack Norwegian reindeer with biological weapons during World War I. These efforts, which were aimed at hindering the use of reindeer as draught animals to transport British supplies across northern Norway to Russia, were not an isolated incident but part of an ambitious German program directed against animals in neutral trading partners of the Allied forces during 1915-18. Germany sent secret agents armed with bacteria that cause anthrax and glanders to Argentina, Norway, Romania, Spain, and the U.S. with instructions to infect shipments of horses, mules, cattle, and sheep bound for the Allies.

Nerve Agents Degraded by Enzymatic Foams. LeJeune, Keith E; Wild, James R; Russell, Alan J. *Nature*. v. 395 no6697 p. 27-8 S 3 '98

A safe, environmentally acceptable way of conducting wide-area decontamination of nerve agents is reported. Organophosphorus hydrolase (OPH), an enzyme that hydrolyzes nerve agents, was incorporated into aqueous foams normally used for fire fighting. OPH was catalytically active within the foams. Multicomponent enzyme foams could be produced through the incorporation of several enzymes of varying specificity.

How to Make Microbes Safer. Pearson, Graham S., *Nature*. v. 394 no6690 p. 217-18 Jl 16 '98

Closer links between international efforts to protect society from natural and engineered microorganisms and efforts to prevent the threat of microorganisms from biological weapons are required. There is a general awareness of the dangers posed by diseases such as Ebola and spongiform encephalitis, and there is concern about the consequences of genetic engineering, notably of foodstuffs. In a different sphere, there is concern about the deliberate use of microorganisms in war or terrorist attacks. A coordinated effort is needed to reap the undoubted benefits of biotechnology while addressing these fears. There are common objectives shared by the current negotiations in Montreal, Canada, to develop protocols on the peaceful use of microorganisms and those taking place in Geneva, Switzerland, on their unlawful military use. There are synergistic benefits to be gained for health and environmental safety and international security by the strengthening of the biological weapons convention.

Deadly Relic of the Great War: Recovery of B. Anthracis in Museum Exhibit in Norway. Redmond, Caroline; Pearce, Martin J; Manchee, Richard J. *Nature.* v. 393 no6687 p. 747-8 Je 25 '98

It has been confirmed that an 80-year-old exhibit from World War I, discovered in a police museum in Trondheim, Norway, contained Bacillus anthracis. The exhibit was a glass bottle containing 2 lumps of sugar, in one of which was embedded a sealed glass capillary tube containing the bacterial spores. The presence of anthrax was confirmed using both culture and PCR techniques.

South Africa's Truth Commission Reveals Bioweapons Plot. Cherry, Michael. *Nature.* v. 393 no6687 p. 724 Je 25 '98

The Truth and Reconciliation Commission in South Africa has heard evidence of a plot to develop biological and chemical weapons under the previous government. The research effort, which was conducted by the South African Defence Force, included efforts to develop drug-laced tear gas and supply poisoning agents. A front company, Roodeplaat Research Laboratories, was also briefed to develop research projects that included the selective poisoning of people based on skin pigmentation, the development of a vaccine to diminish black fertility, and the cultivation of cholera and anthrax organisms.

Poxvirus Dilemmas: Monkeypox, Smallpox, and Biologic Terrorism. Breman, Joel G; Henderson, D. A. *New England Journal of Medicine.* v. 339 no8 p. 556-9 Ag. 20 '98.

All known stocks of variola (smallpox) virus should be destroyed as soon as possible. Eighteen years ago, the WHO's International Commission for the Certification of Smallpox Eradication concluded that the global eradication of smallpox had been achieved. In 1980, the commission recommended that "all institutions maintaining stocks of variola virus destroy or transfer these stocks to WHO collaborating centers equipped with adequate security." There is some argument for keeping stocks of smallpox virus. Smallpox vaccine protects against human monkeypox, and there have been recent reports of outbreaks of possible cases of monkeypox in the Democratic Republic of the Congo (Zaire). However, suggestions that monkeypox might replace smallpox as a serious epidemic threat are unsubstantiated. A more serious consideration is the very real threat posed by the possible use of smallpox as a terrorist weapon. As a large proportion of the population now has no immunity to smallpox, its use as a biologic weapon would be catastrophic. There-fore, the benefits of destroying all remaining stocks outweigh any possible use.

Questions First, Bombs Later: U.S. Missile Attack on the Sudan Factory Was the Wrong Approach. MacKenzie, Debora. *New Scientist*. v. 159 no2152:p51 S 19 '98

The writer disputes the legality and the wisdom of the U.S. bombing of the Shifa factory in Sudan. According to International law, nations are required to investi-gate such situations before they take action, and now the question of whether that factory was making nerve gas or not will never be answered.

Bioarmageddon: Major Cities Are Not Prepared to Deal with Biological Weap-ons. MacKenzie, Debora. *New Scientist*. v. 159 no2152:p. 42-6 S 19 '98

Experts met in Stockholm, Sweden, in May 1998 to discuss the terrorist threat of biological attack on civilians. The threat that terrorists may someday turn to this form of attack is no longer in doubt, as they would have little trouble in acquiring biological weapons. Novel antibioweapon technologies are needed to limit the dev-astation and provide civilian defence.

Death in the Air: Sniffer Plane Flies into Biowarfare Danger Zones. Guterman, Lila. *New Scientist*. v. 159 no2151p.11 S 12 '98

A team of researchers at the Naval Research Laboratory in Washington, D.C., has developed a sensor capable of monitoring the air for signs of biological weapons. The sensor is mounted in a 19-kilogram radio-controlled aircraft with a wingspan of about 4 meters. The device was tested using a harmless bacterium, which it detected in a time of between 5 and 20 minutes at temperatures between 6[degree]C and 24[degree]C. The craft can be sent into possible danger zones to send back data on any biowar bacteria it detects.

Back to Plague Us: Russian Spy-Hydrologist Sergei Volkov, 1979 Anthrax Out-break, and Germ Warfare. MacKenzie, Debora. *New Scientist*. v. 159 no2144 p. 65 Jl 25 '98

The incident of Russian hydrologist Sergei Volkov turning up at a conference on biological weapons in Stockholm, Sweden, in May with a theory about the 1979 anthrax outbreak in an industrial city in the Urals and later claiming he was spying for the KGB illustrates how little is known about Russian germ warfare capabilities.

Biowarfare Sleuths: Online Network of Doctors Monitor Epidemics to Expose Violators of the UN Biological Weapons Convention. Knight, Jonathan. *New Sci-entist*. v. 158 no2139 p. 24 Je 20 '98

A new Internet database could expose violators of the UN ban on military use of biological agents. Al Zelicoff, an expert on biological warfare programs, of Sandia Laboratories, New Mexico, has set up a database to which doctors can post details of outbreaks of disease, allowing the monitoring of current disease trends and epidemiological detection of the probable source of unusual outbreaks. The system's success is dependent on the involvement of thousands of clinics worldwide, but it offers more potential than current methods.

Chemical Hypocrisy: U.S. to Pass Bill Which Will Undermine Chemical Weapons Treaty. Kenzie, Debora. *New Scientist.* v. 158 no2133 p. 5 My 9 '98

A bill that incorporates the UN Chemical Weapons Convention into American law contains provisions allowing the U.S. to exclude UN weapons inspectors from its territory at any time. Critics assert that this is similar to Iraq's efforts to restrict UN weapons inspectors. Supporters of the bill, however, maintain that the provision will probably never be used.

Nowhere to Hide. Boyce, Nell. *New Scientist.* v. 157 no2126 p. 4 Mr 21 '98

Cities in the U.S. are starting a series of drills to work out how they might respond to the threat of bioterrorism. In New York City, officials have completed their first simulated anthrax attack and there are more simulations planned in the future. The results of these trials will be used as a model for further simulations in up to 120 cities across the country. Baltimore has also been selected to host detailed simulations of chemical attacks. Unlike previous simulations, the New York and Baltimore drills involve "field" exercises, but experts in the containment of infectious disease are still worried that current efforts are not enough.

Strike at Will: the More We Prepare for Bioterrorist Attacks, the Worse it All Seems. *New Scientist.* v. 157 no2126 p. 3 Mr 21 '98

The writer discusses the difficulties associated with preparing for attacks on cities by terrorists equipped with biological weapons. In many large cities throughout the world, emergency services have made plans to deal with bioterrorist attacks. Despite these plans, there are real worries that no one can really predict just what type of incident could come next and how to cope with it effectively. The fact remains that many deadly agents are available from hospitals or laboratories which could, in the hands of anyone with some kind of university level knowledge of microbiology, be made in useful amounts.

Detecting Battlefield Toxins. Schlesinger, Hank. *Popular Science.* v. 253 no4:45 O '98

With the Chemical-Biological Mass Spectrometer, Oak Ridge National Laboratory is hoping to make the detection of chemical and biological weapons more reliable. Battlefields do not mimic pristine laboratory conditions, making it hard for instruments to tell the difference between potentially lethal agents and nonlethal bacteria and chemicals. The new unit, which is set to enter production in 2001, will be capable of detecting a large number of chemical and biological weapons, including bacteria, toxins, and viruses.

Biological Weapons Control. Rath, Johannes; Jank, Bernhard; Doblhoff Dier, Otto. *Science.* 282:2194-5 D 18 '98

A letter comments on Thomas P. Monath and Lance K. Gordon's discussion of on-site inspections in biological weapons control, which appeared in the November 20 issue. The writers discuss the value of on-site inspections and sampling as addressed by an international symposium held at the Institute for Applied Microbiology in Vienna, Austria, in May 1998. A response is included.

Strengthening the Biological Weapons Convention. Monath, Thomas P; Gordon, Lance K. *Science.* 282:1423 N 20 '98

One of the most important debates on the Biological and Toxin Weapons Convention (BTWC) concerns on-site inspections. Negotiated during the height of the cold war, the BTWC has no international compliance regime to support its extensive prohibitions against the development, production, stockpiling, and arming of offensive biological weapons. The United States cannot hope to strengthen the BTWC by imposing a compliance protocol while refusing to fully comply itself, but some U.S. pharmaceutical companies have raised legitimate concerns about the risks to confidential business information. Although inspections by the U.S. FDA and Western European national drug control authorities are familiar and unintimidating, concerns have been raised over the unusual objective and potentially intrusive nature of weapons inspections, as well as a possible breach of confidentiality and patent laws.

Arms Control Enters the Biology Lab. Gavaghan, Helen. *Science.* v. 281 no5373 p. 29-30 Jl 3 '98

An enforcement protocol of the Biological and Toxic Weapons Convention (BTWC) could affect some biotechnology companies and academic microbiologists. The treaty, originally negotiated in 1972, did not place a high priority on verification of compliance. Revelations about the biological weapons programs of the former Soviet Union and Iraq have prompted both the Clinton administration and the European Union to push for a compliance protocol to be agreed by the end of 1998. Under such a protocol, facilities that handle potentially worrisome types of biological agents might be obliged to file reports detailing the materials they possess and undergo regular inspections. At a recent meeting in Geneva, many diplomats and arms control experts spoke of creating a combination of "triggers" that would minimize the number of facilities that fall under the treaty by excluding those that possess and produce pathogens for exclusively civilian uses.

Escape from Moscow: Smallpox Virus Eradication, Soviet Biological Warfare Program and World Health Organization. Orent, Wendy. *The Sciences.* v. 38 no3 p. 26-31 My/Je '98

Smallpox, once believed to be on the verge of extinction, continued to be produced by a secret Soviet biological-warfare program. In 1980, the World Health Organization appointed the United States and the Soviet Union to guard what were at the time thought to be the only remaining stocks of the virus. Former Russian biological-warfare expert Ken Alibek, who defected to the West in 1992, said the Soviet Union reproduced tons of smallpox and used it in a lethal aerosol as part of a massive biological-warfare program. The writer examines the reasons for the intended destruction of those last stocks of the virus held in Russia and America, even though tons of the virus are still thought to exist in Russia and elsewhere.

Killer at Large?: Editorial on WHO's Smallpox Virus Eradication, Soviet Biological Warfare Program, and Trust. Brown, Peter G. *The Sciences.* v. 38 no3 p. 4 My/Je '98

Years after the World Heath Organization declared the smallpox virus eradicated from humans, the USSR continued to grow tons of smallpox and prepare it to be installed in refrigerated missiles. The main source of this information is Ken Alibek, a former first deputy director of the Soviet biological-weapons program, who defected to America in 1992. The writer suggests steps that both U.S. and Russian scientists should take to keep the flow of information on subjects like smallpox as open as possible.

Saddam Hussein's City of the Damned: Gassing of Halabja in 1988. Gosden, Christine. *Times Higher Education Supplement.* no1332 p. 19 My 15 '98

The writer reports on a trip to Halabja, which was gassed by Saddam Hussein in 1988, and describes how she was appalled by people's continuing agony and how little is known about the effects of deadly chemical agents.

Index